Surg Gabriel Grant • Col Lewis A. Grant • Cpl William Graul • Pvt John Gray • Sgt ████████████ne • Cpl George Green • Pvt Abraham Greenawalt • Maj Oliver D. Greene • Pvt Joseph ████████ • Ignatz Gresser • Lt James H. Gribben • Pvt Samuel Grimshaw • Col James G. Grindl██████████ • Pvt Thomas Guinn • Pvt Nathaniel Gwynne . . . . Pvt John Hack • Sgt ███████████ • Cpl Osgood T. Hadley • Pvt Asel Hagerty • Sgt John H. Haight • Cpl Sidney Haight • Chap Francis B. Hall • Cpl Newton H. Hall • 2nd Lt H. Seymour Hall • Pvt Nathan M. Hallock • Sgt Henry A. Hammel • Chap Milton L. Haney • Pvt Edward R. Hanford • Pvt Joseph Hanks • Sgt Marcus A. Hanna • Cpl Milton Hanna • Cpl Moses C. Hanscom • Lt Col Douglas Hapeman • Pvt John H. Harbourne • Pvt Henry M. Hardenbergh • 1st Lt Abram P. Haring • Cpl Amzi D. Harmon • Sgt Ephraim W. Harrington • Pvt George W. Harris • Sgt James H. Harris • 1st Lt Moses Harris • Pvt Sampson Harris • Sgt John W. Hart • Pvt William E. Hart • Col John F. Hartranft • Cpl Harry Harvey • Sgt Maj Frank W. Haskell • Sgt Marcus M. Haskell • Capt Smith H. Hastings • Brig Gen John P. Hatch • Sgt John H. Havron • 1st Lt Gardner C. Hawkins • Cpl Martin J. Hawkins • Sgt Maj Thomas Hawkins • Cpl Harris S. Hawthorn • Cpl Asbury F. Haynes • Pvt John H. Hays • Pvt George W. Healey • 1st Lt Joseph Hedges • Capt William L. Heermance • Sgt Henry Heller • Pvt David H. Helms • Col Guy V. Henry • Sgt James Henry • Col William W. Henry • Pvt Pitt B. Herington • Lt Col Francis J. Herron • Col Francis S. Hesseltine • Pvt Joseph C. Hibson • Sgt Dennis W. Hickey • Cpl Nathan E. Hickok • Pvt Charles Higby • Sgt Thomas J. Higgins • Cpl Patrick Highland • Capt Edward Hill • Cpl Henry Hill • 1st Lt James Hill • Sgt James Hill • Mus Benjamin F. Hilliker • Pvt William G. Hills • Sgt Alfred B. Hilton • Sgt Maj William B. Hincks • Pvt Addison J. Hodges • Cpl Henry Hoffman • Capt Thomas W. Hoffman • Cpl Franklin Hogan • Pvt William P. Hogarty • Pvt Daniel I. Holcomb • Pvt James Holehouse • Cpl Lemuel F. Holland • Sgt Maj Milton M. Holland • 1st Sgt Lovilo N. Holmes • Pvt William T. Holmes • 1st Sgt Charles M. Holton • 1st Sgt Edward A. Holton • Color Sgt Conrad Homan • 1st Lt George W. Hooker • Cpl William B. Hooper • Cpl Charles F. Hopkins • Sgt Thomas Horan • Capt Samuel B. Horne • Drum William H. Horsfall • Pvt Solomon J. Hottenstine • Pvt Ira Hough • Capt Charles H. Houghton • Pvt George L. Houghton • Comis Sgt William Houlton • Cpl Henderson C. Howard • Pvt Hiram R. Howard • Sgt James Howard • Brig Gen Oliver O. Howard • 1st Sgt Squire E. Howard • Mus Orion P. Howe • Sgt William H. Howe • Capt William S. Hubbell • Pvt Aaron R. Hudson • Cpl John Hughey • Cpl Oliver Hughs • Lt Col Henry S. Huidekoper • Pvt Lewis T. Hunt • Sgt Charles A. Hunter • Pvt John C. Hunterson • 1st Sgt Theodore Hyatt • Maj Thomas W. Hyde • Capt Samuel Hymer . . . . Sgt Charles H. Ilgenfritz • Cpl Lorenzo D. Immell • Pvt Lewis J. Ingalls • Cpl Leonidas H. Inscho • Capt Francis Irsch • 1st Sgt Patrick Irwin . . . . 1st Sgt Frederick R. Jackson • Sgt Maj Eugene P. Jacobson • Pvt Isaac James • Cpl Miles James • 1st Sgt Walter Jamieson • Sgt James Jardine • Sgt Benjamin H. Jellison • Pvt James T. Jennings • 1st Lt Erastus W. Jewett • Pvt William John • Pvt Franklin Johndro • Cpl Elisha Johns • Pvt Henry T. Johns • Pvt Andrew Johnson • Cpl Follett Johnson • Pvt John Johnson • 1st Lt Joseph E. Johnson • Maj Ruel M. Johnson • Pvt Samuel Johnson • Sgt Wallace W. Johnson • Pvt David Johnston • Mus Willie Johnston • Pvt David Jones • 1st Sgt William Jones • Cpl Absalom Jordan • 1st Lt Simeon T. Josselyn • 1st Sgt Francis W. Judge . . . . Sgt John Kaiser • Cpl Luther Kaltenbach • Cpl John Kane • Pvt Peter Kappesser • Sgt Leopold Karpeles • Cpl August Kauss • Sgt Maj Joseph Keele • Sgt Joseph S. Keen • Pvt Joseph Keene • Pvt Andrew J. Kelley • Capt George V. Kelley • Sgt Leverett M. Kelley • 1st Sgt Alexander Kelly • Sgt Daniel Kelly • Pvt Thomas Kelly • 1st Sgt Joseph Kemp • 1st Sgt William W. Kendall • Pvt John Kennedy • Sgt John S. Kenyon • Pvt Samuel P. Kenyon • Cpl John Keough • Pvt James Kephart • Capt Thomas R. Kerr • Sgt John Kiggins • Pvt Joseph Kimball • Cpl John M. Kindig • Maj Horatio C. King • 1st Lt Rufus King, Jr. • Cpl John Kinsey • Maj Dennis T. Kirby • Capt Jonathan C. Kirk • Pvt Harry Kline • Pvt Charles H. Kloth • Cpl Charles H. Knight • Pvt William Knight • Pvt Abiather J. Knowles • 2nd Lt Edward M. Knox • 1st Lt Jacob Koogle • Mus John S. Kountz • Pvt Theodore L. Kramer • Pvt George Kretsinger • 2nd Lt Andrew Kuder • Lt Jeremiah Kuder . . . . Pvt Joseph S. Labill • Pvt George Ladd • Sgt William Laing • Ch Bugler James P. Landis • Pvt Morgan D. Lane • 1st Lt Aaron S. Lanfare • Mus J. C. Julius Langbein • Cpl Smith Larimer • Cpl James W. Larrabee • 1st Sgt Gaines Lawson • Capt Henry W. Lawton • Sgt Edwin Leonard • Pvt William E. Leonard • Pvt Frank Leslie • Pvt Benjamin Levy • Capt De Witt Clinton Lewis • Cpl Henry Lewis • Cpl Samuel E. Lewis • Capt Adolphe Libaire • Pvt John Lilley • Sgt Henry F. W. Little • Cpl George H. Littlefield • 1st Lt Josiah O. Livingston • Pvt Lewis Locke • Capt John Lonergan • Pvt William H. Longshore • Pvt Joseph Lonsway • Mus William Lord • Comis Sgt Andrew J. Lorish • Col George M. Love • 1st Sgt George M. Lovering • Pvt Cyrus B. Lower • Pvt Robert A. Lower • Pvt George Loyd • Pvt George W. Lucas • Sgt Moses A. Luce • Capt William Ludgate • Pvt Carl Ludwig • Sgt Alphonso M. Lunt • Cpl Franklin W. Lutes • Pvt James H. Luther • Cpl Gotlieb Luty • Qm Sgt Joel H. Lyman • Cpl Frederick A. Lyon . . . . 1st Lt Arthur MacArthur, Jr. • Pvt Michael Madden • Sgt James Madison • Drum William Magee • Sgt Jeremiah Mahoney • 1st Sgt Harry J. Mandy • Pvt Richard C. Mangam • Pvt Joseph S. Manning • 1st Lt William Marland • Sgt Charles Marquette • Sgt Albert Marsh • Pvt Charles H. Marsh • Sgt George Marsh • Sgt George Martin • Lt Sylvester H. Martin • Sgt Elihu H. Mason • 1st Sgt William H. Mathews • Cpl John C. Matthews • Pvt Milton Matthews • Pvt Henry B. Mattingly • Maj Charles P. Mattocks • Cpl Lowell M. Maxham • Pvt William May • Pvt John B. Mayberry • Pvt William B. Mayes • Pvt George H. Maynard • Cpl Peter McAdams • Sgt Benjamin F. McAlwee • Lt Charles McAnally • 1st Lt William W. McCammon • Pvt Bernard McCarren • Pvt Joseph McCauslin • 1st Lt Charles H. McCleary • Pvt James M. McClelland • Capt Samuel McConnell • Pvt Andrew McCornack • Pvt George E. McDonald • Pvt John Wade McDonald • Pvt Samuel O. McElhinny • Sgt Patrick H. McEnroe • Sgt Daniel McFall • Pvt Edward McGinn • Pvt Wilson McGonagle • Capt Andrew J. McGonnigle • Cpl Owen McGough • Sgt Thomas McGraw • Pvt Patrick McGuire • Cpl Alexander U. McHale • Sgt Charles W. McKay • Col Sgt George McKee • 1st Lt Nineveh S. McKeen • Pvt Michael McKeever • Sgt Nathaniel A. McKown • Capt Martin T. McMahon • Sgt Francis M. McMillen • Cpl John P. McVean • Comis Sgt Walter F. McWhorter • Farrier George E. Meach • Tech Sgt John Meagher • Sgt George W. Mears • Sgt John W. Menter • Lt Col Henry C. Merriam • Cpl James K. Merrifield • Capt Augustus Merrill • Pvt George Merrill • Sgt John G. Merritt • Capt Henry C. Meyer • Col Nelson A. Miles • Pvt Frank Miller • Capt Henry A. Miller • Pvt Jacob C. Miller • Pvt James P. Miller • Cpl John Miller • Pvt John Miller • Capt William E. Miller • Sgt Frank W. Mills • Capt George W. Mindel • 1st Lt Alexander H. Mitchell • Pvt Theodore Mitchell • Cpl John H. Moffitt • Sgt Archibald Molbone • Cpl Patrick Monaghan • Cpl Daniel B. Moore • Pvt George G. Moore • Pvt Wilbur F. Moore • Pvt Delano Morey • Pvt Jerome Morford • Pvt Lewis Morgan • Cpl Richard H. Morgan • Capt Walter G. Morrill • Sgt William Morris • Pvt Francis Morrison • Pvt Benjamin Morse • Sgt Charles E. Morse • Pvt John W. Mostoller • Maj St. Clair A. Mulholland • Cpl Walter L. Mundell • Sgt Harvey M. Munsell • 1st Lt Charles J. Murphy • Sgt Daniel Murphy • Sgt Dennis J. F. Murphy • Pvt James T. Murphy • Pvt John P. Murphy • Lt Col Michael C. Murphy • Mus Robinson B. Murphy • Cpl Thomas Murphy • Cpl Thomas C. Murphy • 1st Sgt Thomas J. Murphy • Pvt George S. Myers • Pvt William H. Myers . . . . Cpl Henry Nash • Pvt Zachariah C. Neahr • Capt Edwin M. Neville • Pvt Marcellus J. Newman • Lt William H. Newman • Capt Henry C. Nichols • 2nd Lt Robert Niven • Sgt John J. Nolan • Sgt Conrad Noll • Pvt Jasper N. North • 2nd Lt Elliott M. Norton • Lt John R. Norton • Sgt Llewellyn P. Norton • Pvt William W. Noyes • Capt Lee Nutting . . . . Capt James R. O'Beirne • Cpl Henry D. O'Brien • Pvt Peter O'Brien • Sgt Albert O'Connor • Pvt Timothy O'Connor • Pvt John O'Dea • 1st Lt Menomen O'Donnell • Sgt Charles Oliver • Capt Paul A. Oliver • Cpl Stephen O'Neill • Pvt John N. Opel • Pvt David Orbansky • Pvt Charles A. Orr • Maj Robert L. Orr • Cpl Jacob G. Orth • Pvt William H. Osborne • Pvt Albert Oss • Pvt Jacob H. Overturf . . . . Pvt Loron F. Packard • Mus George H. Palmer • Cpl John G. Palmer • Col William J. Palmer • Cpl Thomas Parker • Cpl James W. Parks • Pvt Jeremiah Parks • Pvt Jacob Parrott • Pvt Joel Parsons • 1st Lt John H. Patterson

WINNERS OF THE MEDAL OF HONOR

by
DONALD E. COOKE

illustrated by
JACK WOODSON

For
Conspicuous
Gallantry...

C. S. Hammond & Company
Maplewood, New Jersey

Other Titles in the PROFILE Series

Crouthers: Flags of American History

Illustrated Atlas for Young America

McNeer: Profile of American History

Cooke: Atlas of the Presidents

Foreword

The compilation of material for this book was necessarily selective. With more than 3,000 names from which to choose, some basis for selection had to be found. The present work is a representative cross section of the Medal of Honor recipients from each of the principal conflicts in which United States fighting men have been involved, from the Civil War, when the Medal was established, up to and including the conflict in Vietnam. At the same time, as many theaters of war and as many branches of service as possible have been represented. For each story the rank of the man given is the one he held at the time of the incident.

In addition, outstanding peacetime recipients, Charles Lindbergh and William C. Mitchell, have been included, along with a number of unusual cases in a section entitled, *Medal of Honor Oddities*.

Above all, each incident included has been presented here because of its compelling excitement or drama. Hundreds of other stories, equally gripping, could be told about Medal winners. But it is the intent of this volume to show how Americans of many different backgrounds, in a host of tense situations, in different times and in every part of the world — soldiers, sailors, marines and airmen of all grades and ranks — have met the supreme challenge with gallantry and indomitable courage.

For their assistance in gathering material for the book, I wish to express my thanks to the following individuals and organizations:

To the Office of the Chief of Information, Department of the Army; United States Army Department of Documents; United States Department of Navy Information; to McGraw-Hill Book Company for their permission to use material from their book OUTPOST OF FREEDOM by Roger Donlon and Warren Rogers in the writing of the Roger Donlon story; to Charles Scribner's Sons for permission to quote from THE SPIRIT OF ST. LOUIS by Charles Lindbergh in my Lindbergh chapter; to The Macmillan Company for quotations from EDDIE RICKENBACKER by Hans Christian Adamson; to E. P. Dutton & Co. for permission to quote from BILLY MITCHELL by Emile Gauvreau and Lester Cohen; and to Doubleday and Company, Inc. for permission to use a quotation from their book, LITTLE BROWN BROTHER by Leon Wolff in my chapter on Hiram Iddings Bearss and David Dixon Porter.

I have also received invaluable help from the staffs of the Wayne Library, Wayne, Pa., and the Free Library of Philadelphia.

Some fascinating World War II detail has been gleaned from the pages of YANK, the Army Weekly, on whose staff I was privileged to serve in 1942–45.

For their patience, forbearance and active help, a salute to the Publisher's entire staff, to my son, Warren, and to my uncomplaining wife, Margaret.

— D.E.C.

Contents

Winners of the Medal of Honor

Maj William H. Powell • Pvt Albert Power • Cpl Wesley J. Powers • Pvt Joseph R. Prentice • 1st Lt Noble D. Preston • Sgt Hiram W. Purcell • Lt James J. Purman • Sgt Edgar P. Putnam • Cpl Winthrop D. Putnam . . . . Col Matthew S. Quay • Maj James Quinlan . . . . Pvt Peter Rafferty • Pvt Charles F. Rand • Asst Surg George E. Ranney • Pvt Myron H. Ranney • 1st Sgt Alfred Ransbottom • 1st Sgt Edward Ratcliff • Asst Surg Jacob F. Raub • Cpl William H. Raymond

The Medal of Honor

Real heroes don't seek recognition — their acts of bravery generally take place under circumstances which permit no thought of medals or special awards. Sometimes heroism is prompted by the instinct for survival. Sometimes the unnatural excitement of battle drives men to apparently superhuman feats that surprise the performers as much as their witnesses. And, sometimes the deeds are coolly calculated by men who are fully aware of the possible risks and consequences involved. However, regardless of the types of men who become heroes and regardless of their motivations, Medal of Honor winners share certain attributes in common because of the rules established for the award. These rules have been changed and refined over the years, but the basic idea was expressed at the outset by Congressmen responsible for the bill establishing the award.

The Navy Medal was established by Act of Congress and approved by President Lincoln on December 21, 1861. Senator James W. Grimes of Iowa, Chairman of the Senate Naval Committee, had been one of the foremost sponsors of the idea, and it was he who had introduced the bill to Congress. Two months later, Senator Henry Wilson of Massachusetts introduced a resolution in the Senate calling for the award of "medals of honor" to "enlisted men of the Army and Volunteer Forces who shall most distinguish themselves by their gallantry in action, and other soldierlike qualities."

This resolution became law on July 12, 1862, when President Lincoln endorsed it with his signature. On March 3, 1863, its provisions were extended retroactively to the start of the Civil War to include officers. Designs for Navy Medals were prepared at the U.S. Mint in Philadelphia under the direction of James Pollock, and the Army and Navy approved a single final design in 1862. The only difference between the Army and Navy versions of the original Medal was that the ribbon was attached to the Navy Medal by an anchor — the Army Medal by an eagle atop crossed cannon.

The first Army Medals were awarded on March 25, 1863; the first Navy awards were made a few days later, April 3, 1863.

Up to the time of McKinley's administration, rules governing the award were somewhat vague, but on June 26, 1897, the Secretary of War announced a revision of Army regulations defining the Medal of Honor award. Then, in 1904, an act of Congress required that all claims for the Medal be accompanied by official documents describing the exploit in detail and supporting the claim. This act also changed the design of the Army Medal, making it different from the Navy decoration. To protect the Medal, the Government issued its own patent (Serial No. 197,369) and placed it under the jurisdiction of Secretary of War W. H. Taft and his successors in office. When the patent expired in 1918, a bill was drafted forbidding imitation of the Medal's design. This bill was passed by Congress, February 24, 1923.

Another Congressional Act of April 27, 1916, provided for the listing of Medal of Honor winners on an official Roll of Honor. A committee of investigators was appointed and given the right to withdraw the Medal from past recipients if they found, after thorough review, that the exploits involved did not live up to certain standards. This Board of Review studied the entire list of 2,625 Medal winners recorded up to that time, and as a result, 911 names were stricken from the list. The majority of these were from a single Civil War regiment — the 27th Maine Volunteer Infantry — who had received the Medal as an inducement to sign up for an additional tour of duty.

11

Others whom the Board disqualified included William F. (Buffalo Bill) Cody and a Civil War woman surgeon, Mary Walker, the only woman ever granted the privilege of wearing the Medal of Honor.

Prior to 1918, the legal definitions of the award had been subject to varied interpretations. Over the years there had been conflicting Congressional acts, and Boards of Review found themselves confused by a host of precedents, traditions, and regulations. As a result, in 1918, Congress passed a new act in an effort to clear up any confusion concerning the Medal once and for all.

This act established the following points:

1. The President was authorized in the name of Congress to present a Medal of Honor "only to each person who, while an officer or enlisted man of the Army, shall hereafter, in action involving actual conflict with an enemy, distinguish himself conspicuously by gallantry and intrepidity at risk of his life above and beyond the call of duty."

2. Enlisted men who won the Medal were to receive two dollars extra per month in their military pay.

3. The Distinguished Service Cross was established in order to protect the supreme position of the Medal of Honor as the highest award. Through the creation of a secondary medal, the Medal of Honor gained additional prestige.

4. Other medals of lesser importance — the Army Distinguished Service Medal and the Army Silver Star — were also established.

5. Recommendations for these awards were to be made within two years after the exploits occurred, and the Medals were required to be issued within three years.

6. Only one Medal of Honor could be awarded to any one person.

Similar legislation governing the Navy Medal of Honor, the Navy Distinguished Service Medal and the Navy Cross was passed in 1919.

Despite changes in the law, from 1862 forward, the Medal of Honor has represented the Nation's highest award for heroism in war and — occasionally — in peace. It has been the subject of many legends and misconceptions, but the fact is that most recipients have been modest men who have neither exploited it nor sought wide publicity for it.

Being a Medal of Honor hero has its moment of supreme glory when the award is made by a high official, often at a personal audience with the President of the United States. The wearers hold the honor with pride for the rest of their lives. But most of them prefer to cherish the Medal quietly, without subsequent fanfare — not merely out of a sense of modesty, but because public knowledge of the award can actually become a liability. Often so much is expected of a Medal of Honor winner that if he makes even a slight mistake at his job or gets into any kind of financial or marital trouble, he is likely to be subjected to far more adverse criticism and unpleasant publicity than an ordinary citizen.

Medal winners have actually enjoyed few special privileges. Although for many years it was customary for all living wearers to receive a red-carpet invitation to each President's inauguration, even this special recognition was discontinued at President Johnson's inauguration in January, 1965. Invitations were sent, but they failed to include seats of honor with other top-ranking guests, and the traditional tickets to inaugural balls were omitted. Most men who accepted the invitation traveled at their own expense and found their own lodgings.

Medal of Honor winners do rate free transportation on military planes where space is available. They can obtain a Government pension of one hundred dollars a month after age 40, and their sons may obtain appointments to West Point, the Air Force Academy, or Annapolis without a Congressman's endorsement, provided the applicants meet physical and scholarship

12

qualifications. Contrary to a popular notion, Medal recipients wearing the insignia in their lapels do not rate a hand salute from military or naval personnel.

In 1965 there were 283 living Medal of Honor winners. The first award was made in 1863, and since that time 3,171 Medals have been awarded up to and including one to Captain Roger H. C. Donlon, whose heroism in Vietnam, on July 6, 1964, was honored by President Johnson in December of that year. The largest number of Medals was awarded during the Civil War, a total of 1,527. Only 123 were presented in World War I. The Indian Wars produced 541 Medalists; the Spanish-American War 123; World War II 430; and Korea 131. A few other awards were made in "interim" engagements, such as the Philippine Insurrec-

tion, and a total of seven Medals have been awarded for peacetime feats of heroism.

The figures tend to indicate that it is more difficult to earn a Medal of Honor now than in the past, and the fact is regulations governing this Nation's highest award have tightened over the years. The care with which legal terminology and restrictions have been worked out in connection with the Medal has made it virtually impossible for an undeserving person to become a recipient. However, no specific regulations can ever give assurance that all genuine heroes will be publicly honored. Undoubtedly there have been thousands of acts of supreme bravery that have gone unrecognized and unrewarded. But it is equally certain that to most of these heroes, courage, like virtue, is its own reward.

13

The First Awards

Andrews Raiders

Like the drums of war, thunder muttered ominously as a group of men conferred at a secret meeting place on the Wartrace Road, near an army camp at Shelbyville, Tennessee. The date was April 7, 1862, a time when the Union was still hoping to end the Civil War with a few quick offensives.

The leader of the twenty-three who gathered at that nocturnal conference was James J. Andrews, a civilian agent who had penetrated the Southern lines on a number of occasions, and who had conceived of a bold plan to disrupt Confederate supplies and re-inforcements.

"You have volunteered for a hazardous mission deep into Confederate territory," Andrews told the group. "The scheme is to commandeer a Confederate train on the Atlanta-Chattanooga line, drive it north, and destroy the track and bridges along the way. We will rendezvous with General Mitchell's forces in Bridgeport, Alabama. Mitchell's objective is to drive a wedge between the Confederate forces."

The audacity of the scheme was beyond anything the volunteers had expected, but none of the men dropped out. The next day they set out in small groups, carrying Confederate money, disguised in civilian clothes and posing as Confederates escaping from a Yankee prison camp. They chose routes that crossed wild country for the most part, and with the exception of two men who were actually pressed into service with the Confederate Army, all reached Marietta, Georgia, where they gathered at the Marietta Hotel. Early on the morning of April 12th at about 5:00 A.M., Andrews and his band of raiders began to drift into the station. They bought tickets for various points along the line, then calmly boarded the Chattanooga train. It was pulled by a handsomely decorated locomotive labeled GENERAL. Without appearing to notice each other, the Andrews party found seats in the forward coach, and the train moved out on schedule.

James Andrews had picked his volunteers with care. Three had been locomotive engineers in civilian life. They were Privates Wilson Brown, William Knight, and Martin J. Hawkins. The rest had been chosen for skills and courage they had demonstrated in previous actions. They were Privates William Bensinger, Robert Buffum, Jacob Parrott, John R. Porter, Samuel Robertson, Samuel Slavens, James Smith, George D. Wilson, John A. Wilson, John Wollam and Mark Wood; also Corporals Daniel Dorsey and William H. Reddick; Sergeant Major Marion A. Ross and Sergeants Elihu Mason, William Pittinger and, finally, John M. Scott.

Without incident, the train reached Big Shanty (now known as Kennesaw) where it stopped to allow the passengers time for breakfast. The Andrews men left the coach on the side away from the station. While an armed sentry from a nearby Confederate army camp watched curiously, the Yankee party deliberately uncoupled the coaches from the first three boxcars. Andrews and Wilson Brown then clambered into the cab of the locomotive while the others boarded the third boxcar. Brown eased open the throttle. With a powerful puffing, the *General* began to move.

The train's crew emerged from the station as the *General* was gathering speed but by the time a handful of soldiers from the camp had been aroused, the locomotive was chugging swiftly down the main track. Shots rang out, but the bullets went wide of the speeding train.

Rain had begun to fall as the stolen train left the station. Soon the sky darkened and the rain came down in torrents. Highly elated, the Andrews raiders sped north into the storm. Since they could see no sign of

14

pursuit, they stopped after traveling a few miles, cut telegraph wires, and loaded the rear car with crossties. It was their plan to use these as track barricades and as kindling to burn bridges. At Etowah, the *General* passed a siding where the locomotive *Yonah* stood puffing steam. The raiders debated the advantages of attacking the *Yonah* crew and putting the locomotive out of commission, but they felt that it was more important to keep moving north. They waved to the *Yonah* crew and sped on. This proved to be one of their fatal blunders.

They continued to cut telegraph wires, and at one point they paused long enough to rip up a length of track. The April rain fell steadily.

Farther along the line they stopped at Cass Station for wood and water. From all appearances, the station provided everything they would need to continue their journey. Just beyond a low shed was a water tank. Nearby was a large stack of firewood.

The stationmaster came striding angrily toward them from the shed. Jim Andrews met the situation with his usual disarming courtesy. "The train from Atlanta will be along in a little while," he said. "This is a special powder train carrying ammunition to Beauregard's forces at Corinth."

Stationmaster Russell eyed Andrews and the others with obvious suspicion, but as the crew continued unconcernedly to pile wood in the tender, acting for all the world as though it was their duty to get the job done with dispatch, Russell began to relax.

Andrews pressed his advantage. "This powder mission was organized in a mighty big hurry," he drawled. "Our information on southbound trains is sketchy, but they told me you could give me the schedule."

Convinced that everything possible must be done to get powder and ammunition to General Beauregard, the stationmaster handed Andrews a complete schedule of train movements on the line ahead. In a few minutes, the *General's* water tank was full and the tender was piled high with wood. With a jaunty wave to Stationmaster Russell, they pulled out of Cass and picked up speed.

The next few miles were uneventful, but then they approached the busy Kingston yards. This was an important railroad junction. Switches would have to be crossed, there would be switchmen, train crews and yardmen, none of whom would be expecting Andrews' "powder train." According to their schedule, a southbound freight should be on a Kingston siding, waiting for the *General* to pass through.

But as they came in sight of the junction   15

they could see that the siding was empty. This meant that they would have to wait for the southbound train to pass through. There would be questions, of course, but there was no help for it.

Brown throttled down the *General,* and they approached the station slowly. A number of passengers, waiting on the platform, picked up luggage as the stolen train approached, but their faces showed disappointment when they saw that there were no passenger cars.

Before the *General* had come to a full stop, Andrews swung to the platform and strode purposefully to the telegraph office. He threw the surprised telegraph operator into a state of confusion by an aggressive approach.

"Do you want this load of ammunition to blow up right here in the station?" he demanded. "You'll have to open the siding for us until the freight goes through, then get us out of here fast."

The telegraph operator grudgingly complied with Andrews' instructions. But when the southbound train arrived, it carried a red flag on the last car, indicating that another train was following. To the annoyance of the Andrews raiders, they were delayed still longer. It turned out that all Confederate trains on the line were being ordered to move south because the Yanks were pushing Beauregard's troops back. When the second train passed, it, too, carried a red flag. But this time, Andrews refused to wait longer. He persuaded the switchman to open the siding switch and let the *General* move out onto the main line. It was his plan to try to reach the siding at Adairsville ahead of the next southbound train.

More than an hour had been lost during this tense ordeal at Kingston. The raiders were worried about pursuit, though they had no way of knowing that the conductor of the stolen train, William A. Fuller, had never given up the chase. He had followed on a handcar to the siding where the *Yonah*

was waiting and, with several soldiers, had chased the raiders to Kingston on the commandeered locomotive. Near Kingston the determined conductor had also been stopped by the southbound freights, but undaunted, he and his Confederate troops ran to a point on a branch line half a mile away, where a train for Rome, Georgia, had been waiting to receive mail from the *General.* Now, using the Rome locomotive, Fuller was again in hot pursuit.

The Andrews raiders stopped the *General* to tear up a stretch of track, but they had scarcely started the job when Fuller's engine came in sight. As shots rang out, the raiders leaped back into their stolen train, and a desperate race was under way. Near the town of Adairsville, engineer William Knight slowed down because their information indicated that a southbound passenger train was due.

"Maybe we can outrace the express to the next siding," suggested Brown. "If we wait here, the Rome locomotive will catch us, sure."

Knight opened the throttle wide; the *General* barreled down the line at tremendous speed. In a few minutes they had traveled nearly ten miles. The siding came in sight, but so did the oncoming express. Knight blew the whistle frantically until the approaching train heeded the warning, stopped, then backed up far enough for the *General* to enter the siding.

The express moved on and passed the pursuing Rome locomotive beyond Adairsville. When Fuller was stopped by a barricade of crossties, the Confederates abandoned their locomotive and continued the chase in the *Texas,* which they found on a siding a little farther down the line. Meanwhile Andrews and his men tried desperately to fire the bridges along the route, but the torrential rain extinguished the flames. They uncoupled two of the boxcars, hoping to block the track and to increase their own speed. But Fuller merely pushed the loose cars ahead of him. Eventually the *Gen-*

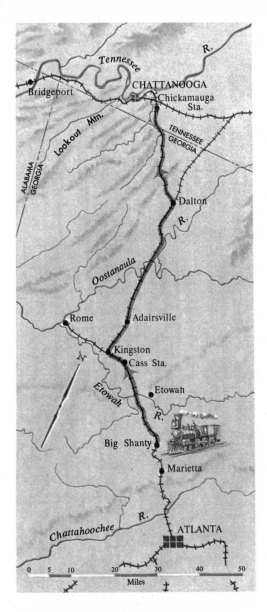

Andrews raiders abandoned the locomotive and escaped into the surrounding woods, every one of them was captured within a few days. They were imprisoned at Chattanooga and Atlanta. Andrews escaped but was recaptured. Seven of the group, including James Andrews, were hanged at the Atlanta prison. For some unexplained reason, the rest, however, were spared. They remained in prison until the following October, when they attempted a daring jail break. They attacked the jailer, knocked him unconscious, took his keys and got away. Knight and Brown found their way back to their regiment, Hawkins and Dorsey joined a Federal force in Kentucky, while Porter and Wollam succeeded in making their way to Corinth.

Six others — Bensinger, Buffum, Mason, Pittinger, Reddick and Parrott were less fortunate. Recaptured and put in irons, they again endured atrocious prison conditions until March 1863, when they were exchanged for six Confederate prisoners and were summoned to Washington. On March 25th, these six men became the first recipients of the recently created Medal of Honor. In an interview with Secretary of War Stanton, each man was given $100. Private Jacob Parrott, youngest of the group, was asked by Secretary Stanton if he would like to go to school. Although Stanton offered enough money to provide an excellent education, young Parrott is said to have declined the offer, saying he wanted to fight the Rebels until they were beaten.

Stanton then showed them the newly struck Medals, presenting the first one to Private Parrott. As he shook hands all around, he announced that each of the surviving Andrews raiders had been given a first lieutenancy. In all of the Medal's illustrious history, no more daring exploit would be recorded yet, ironically, the courageous leader and author of the scheme, James Andrews, received no formal recognition for his valor — only the Confederate hangman's rope.

eral's fuel began to run low. At a covered bridge near Chickamauga Station they set the remaining boxcar afire and left it blazing on the bridge. This maneuver might have succeeded, but the soaked timbers of the bridge covering refused to ignite. The pursuing *Texas* pushed the burning car off the bridge, the Confederates upended it from the track, and the chase was resumed.

After a harrowing ninety miles, the valiant *General* ran out of fuel. Although the

17

Daniel E. Sickles, Maj. Gen., USA

". . . most conspicuous gallantry on the field"

The most terrible battle of America's most terrible war began in the heat of July 1863, and continued for three of the bloodiest days in the history of warfare. At Gettysburg, the climactic battle of the Civil War, the South nearly broke through Northern defenses, but finally Lee's offensive power was smashed.

On July 1, a patrol of Federal cavalry made first contact with the advancing Confederate army when it encountered a Southern force northwest of Gettysburg. So overwhelming was the Confederate strength that the Union cavalry unit was forced to call for help from First Corps infantry. The Confederates continued to pour men into the front until the entire right wing of Federal defense collapsed. Bearing the brunt of this attack was the Eleventh Corps, veterans of Chancellorsville. They were badly mauled by Stonewall Jackson's famed troops, commanded by Richard Ewell.

While the Southerners took up positions on Seminary Ridge, the Union troops retreated through the streets of Gettysburg and prepared to make a stand on Cemetery Hill south of the town. In this first day's action, the ill-fated Eleventh Corps had lost between four and five thousand men captured, and sustained 7,000 casualties. Not more than 5,500 men remained to defend Cemetery Ridge and the Round Tops.

This was one of the crucial turning points of the war. Realizing that the Union position was vulnerable, General Lee ordered Ewell to take Cemetery Hill "if practicable." But Ewell did not interpret Lee's gentlemanly phrasing, asking him to take the hill "if practicable" as an order to attack. At any rate, General Ewell held back, Lee failed to issue a positive order, and the delay gave Union General Meade time to bring up re-inforcements shortly after dusk. Meade set up his headquarters

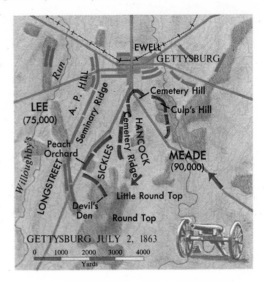

GETTYSBURG JULY 2, 1863

on the protected slope of Cemetery Ridge.

As a misty light dawned on the second day, Union forces were steeling themselves for the inevitable Confederate attack. Culp's Hill, where Meade was expecting the main assault, was on the right. General Hancock, in command of the Second Corps, held the center, with his men spread out along Cemetery Ridge; while on the left, at Devil's Den, was the Third Corps under General Daniel E. Sickles. To the surprise of the Northern commander, Lee made his attack on both Federal flanks, instead of on the right only, as Meade had anticipated. But Confederate General Longstreet delayed getting his attack on the Union left moving at full strength until between 3:00 and 4:00 in the afternoon. During the morning respite, after a conference with Generals Meade and Hunt, General Sickles shifted his position to higher ground in a peach orchard and wheat field half a mile or so in front of Cemetery Ridge. This dangerously separated his troops from Hancock's Second Corps, and his action became one of the most controversial points in the Battle of Gettysburg. Scarcely had Sickles com-

pleted this maneuver when Confederates charged Devil's Den and rushed up the boulder-strewn slope of the undefended Little Round Top — a height which Meade had wanted Sickles to hold. The Southern charge was met by a desperate counter-attack of Fifth Corps units under General G. K. Warren, who managed to protect the position temporarily.

Now Longstreet sent a division into the gap between Sickles' force and the Second Corps. In the peach orchard and the wheat field, a wild battle developed. The sector became a horrible nightmare of hand-to-hand fighting, crashing muskets and the screams of wounded men. Whether or not Sickles had made a tactical blunder, his courage in the face of adversity remains un-questioned. In the midst of this melée, Dan Sickles sat astride his horse, waving his sword and urging his men to stand fast. Suddenly he was knocked from his mount, his knee badly shattered by grapeshot. Meanwhile, the Union artillery up on the ridge had begun to find the range against the waves of Confederate troops charging up the slopes.

Despite the devastating effect of the artil-lery barrage, the Third Corps men had begun to falter. A rumor was rapidly spreading that their popular leader, Dan Sickles, had been killed, and the news served to dampen their spirits and they be-gan to fall back.

But though Sickles was in great pain, he was not dead. Seeing what was happening, he ordered a stretcher brought, and had some men assigned to carry him about the field. Disregarding the excruciating pain of his shattered leg, he propped himself up on his stretcher and encouraged his men.

Although Sickles' Third Corps was nearly destroyed, elements from the Union center counterattacked, preventing a major Confederate breakthrough on the Union left flank. When dusk fell on the second day of Gettysburg, the high ground on Cemetery Ridge was still in Union hands.

After Sickles was carried to a field hos-pital following the Battle of the Wheat Field, surgeons amputated the shattered leg.

General Lee and the Confederates had lost most of their opportunities to smash through Federal defenses. On the third day, Lee gambled everything in one vast frontal assault, and lost. From then on, the South-ern army could only retreat into their own territory and fight delaying actions until the final surrender at Appomattox.

Daniel Sickles was awarded the Medal of Honor on October 30, 1897, for his hero-ism at Gettysburg.

19

William B. Poole, QM, USN
James Saunders, QM, USN

". . . gallantry under fire"

For months, Union ships had been haunted by a Confederate terror of the seas — the *Alabama* which had been secretly built for the Confederacy at Birkenhead, England. With incredible skill, her captain, Raphael Semmes, eluded the warships of the Federal Navy. But all too frequently he had the *Alabama* on hand to intercept a commercial ship, with valuable cargo, on its way to a Northern port. In a two-year period between 1862 and 1864, the raider had captured or sunk more than fifty Union ships with cargoes valued at six and a half million dollars. Despite the best efforts of the U.S. Navy, no Northern vessel had ever engaged the *Alabama* in combat. Suddenly word came to Captain John A. Winslow of the Federal sloop *Kearsarge,* that the enemy ship had been forced to put into port at Cherbourg, France, for repairs. A few days after the *Alabama* docked, on June 14, 1864, the *Kearsarge* appeared off the coast of France where she waited for the Rebel vessel to make for the sea.

On board the Union warship, Quartermaster William B. Poole nervously anticipated the approaching battle. Should it be his turn at the helm when the battle began, he would bear an awful responsibility. Another quartermaster aboard the *Kearsarge* sat in the brig, more concerned about being court-martialed. This was James Saunders who had gotten himself into trouble on a recent shore leave in Holland, where he had been involved in a brawl.

On the morning of June 19th the *Alabama* appeared to be getting up steam. The sky had been overcast and there was still a threat of low clouds and squalls. Captain Winslow, observing the enemy through binoculars felt certain the *Alabama* would attempt to make a run into the teeth of a rain squall. He ordered the *Kearsarge* to be made battle-ready. Gun crews were sent to their stations, decks were cleared and sanded, and, as every able man was needed, James Saunders was released from the brig to take part in the approaching battle.

At about 10:00 A.M. the *Alabama's* sails were suddenly unfurled and the dauntless Confederate ship moved rapidly out to sea. By this time, hundreds of spectators had gathered on the bluffs along the French coast. They could clearly see the two warships as they began to circle and close in for an engagement. The threatening skies had largely cleared, but the natural haze was soon to be replaced by clouds of acrid gunsmoke. It was close to 11:00 A.M. when the first broadsides thundered.

Aboard the *Kearsarge,* Quartermaster Poole stood calmly at the helm, following the commander's orders and steering in a steadily tightening circle, closing the gap between the two ships. Below, the gun crews sweated in stifling heat, bandannas tied over their foreheads. They ran their guns back from the gun ports, rammed powder charges into the muzzles. The shells were then forced down on top of the charges. After loading, the crews rolled the ponderous

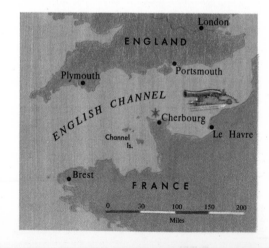

weapons back into place while the gun captains inserted priming wires through breech holes to pierce the powder bags. Next, each gun captain sighted and fired his piece by inserting a lighted swab into the breech. With a roar, the iron monsters recoiled. Though the guns were restrained by ropes, occasionally lines were known to snap and the cannon would smash through the opposite side of the ship, killing and maiming sailors on the way. Meanwhile, enemy shot, flying splinters and shell fragments took their grim toll.

The exchange of firing between the *Kearsarge* and the *Alabama* was so rapid that the booming of cannon became one continuous roll of thunder. At times the dense smoke-clouds completely hid the vessels from the crowds lining the shore. But the *Kearsarge* gun crews far outclassed those on the *Alabama*. Out of some 350 rounds fired by the Confederates, only 25 or 30 were reported to have struck the Union ship, whereas the well-drilled Yankee gunners poured broadside after broadside into the battered *Alabama*. One Confederate shell landed near the *Kearsarge's* helm, hitting the sternpost with a shuddering crash. Still, Poole and Saunders unflinchingly guided the *Kearsarge* in for the kill. Incredibly, the shell never exploded.

The deck of the *Alabama* was littered with dead and wounded as she began to settle, her waterline shattered. After Captain Semmes had directed that a white flag be raised, he threw his sword into the water, then leaped in after it. He was later rescued by an English yacht.

To the men of the *Kearsarge* it was a glorious victory, since they had destroyed the scourge of Union shipping. For their cool courage and skill under heavy direct fire, thirteen members of the gun crews were awarded Medals of Honor. They were: Paymaster's Steward Michael Ahearn, Captain of the Top John F. Bickford, Boatswain's Mate William Bond, Captain of the Forecastle James Haley, Seamen James H. Lee, George H. Harrison, Charles Moore, Joachim Pease and George E. Read; also Boatswain's Mate Thomas Perry, Coxswain Charles A. Reed, Quartermaster William Smith, and Captain of the Top Robert Strahan.

In addition, Quartermasters William B. Poole and James Saunders were awarded the Medal. The battle might easily have been lost at the crucial moment when the sternpost received its direct hit, had they failed to remain steadfast. As an additional reward for his courageous conduct, Saunders' punishment was dropped.

21

Fifteen Awards

". . . constancy and devotion to the flag"

Following the Civil War, the United States was eager to re-establish foreign contacts that had been broken during our nation's tragic internal struggle. At the same time a desire for expansion of trade sent the Navy on diplomatic missions to the Far East. In the nineteenth century the Orient was still veiled in mystery as far as the West was concerned. Least known of all was a land called Korea, the "Hermit Kingdom," from which all foreigners had been barred for nearly 300 years. This exclusiveness stemmed, not from Western exploitation, but from an invasion of warring Japanese and Chinese armies in 1592. At that time, the Koreans had succeeded in driving out the soldiers of both neighboring countries and had vowed to keep its ports and borders closed to all from that day forward.

In 1866 an American sailing vessel, the *General Sherman,* had brashly pushed up the Tae-dong River in Korea. The ship ran aground and was promptly destroyed and its crew massacred by the natives. Two official searching expeditions in 1867 failed to give any clues as to the fate of the vessel.

Finally, in 1871, the United States Asiatic Squadron under Rear Admiral John Rodgers sailed into Korean waters to investigate the incident. Meanwhile, on orders from Washington, the American Minister to China was attempting to negotiate a trade treaty with Korea.

The U.S. warships anchored off Chemulpo (now Inchon) and a number of small boats were sent out by the fleet to survey the estuary of the Han River. They had advanced scarcely a hundred yards when they were fired on by Korean shore batteries. Admiral Rodgers demanded an apology from the Korean heads of state, but having received no reply after waiting ten days, he organized an assault on the Korean forts. Several hundred sailors and Marines,

carrying small arms and light artillery, stormed ashore on June 9, 1871. The landing was supported by fire from the *Monocacy* and the *Palos,* while other ships of the fleet stood by.

Lashed to the ridgerope on the gunwale of the lead launch, Seaman John Andrews made soundings of the unfamiliar channel and gave his reports calmly while cannon and small arms fire whistled on all sides. Still under heavy fire, the Americans scrambled ashore and prepared to attack a complex of fortifications, the principal one being a circular redoubt known as the "Citadel." On the first day the attackers stormed the outlying forts and quickly subdued the defenders.

The Citadel, however, promised to be a tougher challenge. Even rocks were hurled from the parapet. In a hail of bullets, Company D, commanded by a Lieutenant McKee, was the first group to start scaling the ramparts. The men somehow succeeded in climbing to the top of the wall. The first man up was Marine Private Hugh Purvis. He was followed by Lieutenant McKee, Boatswain's Mate Alexander McKenzie and Quatermaster Samuel F. Rogers.

"This way, men!" shouted McKee. The Lieutenant started to run along the wall towards a group of defenders when he fell wounded. Koreans, brandishing swords, rushed at the fallen officer, while McKenzie and Rogers stood over him and fought off the attackers. Almost at once, McKenzie was struck and severely cut on the head by an enemy saber. Rogers was also wounded. Seconds later Private John Coleman rushed to McKenzie's aid. He charged headlong into the press of Koreans, drove them off and dragged McKenzie to safety.

Meanwhile, Private Purvis, together with Corporal Charles Brown, raced to a nearby flagpole and tore down the Korean banner.

With Lieutenant McKee out of action, the company was under the command of Quartermaster Frederick Franklin, who took charge of a chaotic situation with remarkable audacity and skill. He rallied the Americans, drove the remaining Koreans from the wall and directed the first stages of the attack on the inner defenses of the fort. During the ensuing wild hand-to-hand battle, Ship's Carpenter Cyrus Hayden, serving as the American color bearer, climbed to the highest point on the Citadel's ramparts, braved intense gunfire and planted the Stars and Stripes. He then fought off Koreans until assistance came.

One intrepid Marine, Private Michael McNamara, pulled himself over the ledge of the parapet only to come face to face with a Korean soldier. He wrenched an old-time matchlock out of the Korean's hands, felled him and proceeded to club other attackers senseless, swinging the captured matchlock right and left. Private James Dougherty with one bullet wound, found a medical corpsman, had his wound bandaged, and returned to the fight. In the ensuing fight, he was struck several times, but each time he returned to the action.

The Koreans were overcome finally by the furious American assault and their survivors abandoned the forts. For their gallantry, 15 men received Medals of Honor. They were: Seaman John Andrews, Corporal Charles Brown, Private John Coleman, Private James Dougherty, Quartermaster Patrick H. Grace, Carpenter Cyrus Hayden, Landsman William F. Lukes, Boatswain's Mate Alexander McKenzie, Private Michael McNamara, Landsman James F. Merton, Private Michael Owens, Private Hugh Purvis, Quartermaster Samuel F. Rogers and Seaman William Troy.

Although seizure of the forts did not immediately result in a trade treaty, the Koreans were less belligerent afterward.

23

Marion P. Maus, 1st Lt., USA

". . . most distinguished gallantry"

In the Wild West of the 1880's, American troops were involved in some of the bloodiest battles in all United States history. Renegade Indian chiefs, vowing vengeance on the White Man, who had driven them from their hunting grounds, were waging campaigns of terror unmatched in the annals of warfare, and one of the most feared of the savage leaders was the Apache medicine man, Geronimo.

This crafty leader, with several hundred warriors and squaws, had broken out of an Arizona reservation in 1876. He led his people south, across the "ghost line" that divided the United States and Mexico, and disappeared into the craggy Sierra Madre Mountains. From his mountain hideout, he sent raiding parties into Arizona. On one terrible raid, ten Apache braves, led by the youthful chief Josanine, covered over a thousand miles, captured two to three hundred horses and mules, killed thirty-seven white settlers, horribly mutilating the corpses, attacked their own Apache brothers on a peaceful reservation, killing a score of Indians, and returned unscathed to their secret camp in Mexico. Yet they accomplished this bloody work in an area patrolled by over forty companies of infantry, an equal number of troops of cavalry and hundreds of Apache scouts.

At Fort Bowie, Arizona, General George Crook organized an expedition to find and destroy Geronimo. Four white officers were placed in command of a small army of Apache scouts. The first officer was a cautious West Point captain by the name of Emmet Crawford. Next in line was First Lieutenant Marion P. Maus, a tough Indian fighter who had seen considerable action against the Sioux. The only other white men in the expedition were Lieutenants Shipp and Sieber, and a doctor.

Early in December 1885, the ragtag

army of half-naked Indians, astride barebacked ponies, set out from Fort Bowie for the Mexican border. An agreement with the Mexican government permitted U.S. troops to cross the border in pursuit of Indian raiders.

Throughout the march, Captain Crawford showed little enthusiasm for his mission. He allowed Maus to make most of the decisions and gave him full responsibility for trying to maintain some sort of discipline. This was a staggering assignment in itself, for the rebellious braves somehow obtained mescal, a Mexican liquor, and were frequently drunk and disorderly.

Fretting over the slow progress of the expedition, Lieutenant Maus persuaded the captain to let him scout ahead of the main contingent, taking with him a handful of the best men. By now they were deep into the Sierra Madre Mountains and were beset by snow and bitter cold. Early in January, Maus and his advance scouting party stumbled on the trail of Josanine. Eagerly they pressed on into the icy canyons. At night they observed camp fires gleaming

24

high up on the mountain peaks.

Maus waited for the rest of their force to catch up, and on the morning of January 11, 1886, they surrounded Geronimo's camp on the Rio Aros. In a brief battle, they captured the settlement, the women and children, ponies, and supplies. But Geronimo and the survivors escaped while Captain Crawford's Apaches celebrated.

Not long afterward, the American officers were apprised of the approach of a Mexican force. It turned out to be an expedition like their own — an army of Tarahumare Indian scouts led by a few Mexican officers. As a result, a tense situation suddenly developed. The two Indian armies glared at each other while the white officers tried to calm them. Maus and Crawford were calling out to the Mexicans when rifle firing occurred. Some reports say that the first shots came from the Mexicans, but in any case, Captain Crawford was mortally wounded. While Lieutenant Maus carried the wounded captain back to his encampment, the Mexicans likewise retreated, with several of their own men wounded by bullets fired by Crawford's scouts. Then, a voice echoed from the heights above their heads. There, on a rocky promontory, stood Geronimo. Addressing the Apache scouts, he urged them to join his men and slaughter the Tarahumare Indians. Maus quickly turned the explosive situation to his own particular advantage.

"Run for your lives!" he warned the Mexicans. "Go at once, or we will release the Apaches to fight their enemies."

The Mexican officers wasted no time, ordering their force to retreat swiftly down the valley.

By this time, the Apaches were in an ugly mood, and Maus' position was perilous. His captain was mortally wounded, many of his men had been killed in the previous battle, and Geronimo seemed on the verge of persuading the Apaches to join him. The lieutenant's only hope was a show of boldness. When Geronimo asked for a powwow, Maus stood his ground as firmly as the surrounding mountains. To the Indian's demands that his women and children be returned to him, Maus responded with a counter-demand that Geronimo meet with the American commanding general in the spring at an appointed place and that he turn over some hostages to assure the American army's safe return to Fort Bowie.

Geronimo agreed. The eventual result was a lasting peace pact which ended the Apache terror.

Lieutenant Marion Maus was awarded the Medal of Honor for his exploit.

25

Richmond P. Hobson, Lt., USN

". . . by extraordinary courage"

When news of a Cuban insurrection against Spain broke in 1895, a large segment of the United States public was spoiling for a fight. American involvement in international affairs had been on a minor scale for many years, yet the growing strength of the United States made most Americans feel the need to play a dominant role in world affairs. If a national attitude could be described in terms of an individual personality, it might be said that the United States in this period was like a giant who had overcome an inferiority complex and was anxious to show his prowess.

The rebellion in Cuba, reported in colorful terms by the press, provided Americans with the prodding they needed to show their prowess. Soon people were demanding ac-

tion to help the Cubans obtain their freedom. For the better part of three years, the country built up its righteous indignation to national fever pitch, though here and there were some sober thinkers who deplored this warlike enthusiasm. The "Journal of Com-

merce" at one point carried this editorial comment: "What the occasion for all this militant insanity is we do not know . . . Undoubtedly the reconstruction of the navy has done much in this direction . . . Unquestionably naval officers are impatient to use their new fighting machines, and the people have begun to catch the infection of the naval officers."

One of the Navy's "fighting machines" was anchored in Havana harbor in February 1898. It was the battleship *Maine,* sent to Havana to protect U.S. citizens. On the evening of February 15th, the *Maine* blew up. Sabotage was suspected. This incident was the final straw, and on April 25, 1898, Congress formally declared war on Spain.

The Spanish-American War has been jokingly called a "musical comedy war," but to some of the individual soldiers and sailors who saw real action, there was nothing amusing about the experience.

In order to bottle up elements of the Spanish fleet and to prevent the escape of Spanish Admiral Cervera y Topete, U.S. Admiral William T. Sampson decided to run a ship aground at the narrow entrance to Santiago Harbor. For the hazardous task, he selected a young naval constructor named Richmond Pearson Hobson. It was Hobson's responsibility to run an old collier, the U.S.S. *Merrimac,* directly under the muzzles of enemy shore batteries on each side of the harbor entrance and within range also of infantry small arms on shore.

Hobson picked a volunteer crew of six men. They were Gunner's Mate First Class George Charette, Coxswain Osborn Deignan, Watertender Francis Kelly, Chief Master-at-Arms Daniel Montague, Coxswain John Edward Murphy and Machinist First Class George F. Phillips.

Before daylight on the morning of June 3, 1898, this daring crew steamed the *Mer-*

rimac into the harbor. Dark as it was, enemy gunners soon spotted the bulky vessel. As it approached the narrow strait, the Spaniards opened a thunderous artillery barrage which continued for some time. Observers on the United States fleet waited anxiously, and when the firing suddenly ceased, they were certain that the *Merrimac* had been blown to bits and her crew killed. At the first glimmer of dawn, a U.S. cutter approached the area, hoping to pick up survivors, but they could see no sign of the men or of the life raft they had taken with them to make their escape.

The fact was, Lieutenant Hobson and his men had been trying desperately to carry out their mission, though with little success. The *Merrimac* had scarcely come under fire when Coxswain Deignan, who was at the helm, called out, "She won't respond, sir! The tiller ropes have been shot away!" Completely out of control, the vessel drifted beyond the narrows where Hobson had hoped to block the entrance by running aground. In deeper water, with shells still bursting on all sides, Hobson finally managed to sink the ship by detonating two of the torpedoes strapped to the collier's side for just that purpose. As it happened they were in a spot which left ample passageway on each side of the hulk.

The seven volunteers abandoned the *Merrimac* and, still under fire, tried to escape on their life raft. But by this time, light began to dawn. Rifle fire from the beach drove them into the water, where they clung to the raft, keeping it between themselves and the enemy.

Some time later, they had drifted close to shore and were captured and taken aboard a Spanish steam launch.

That afternoon a Spanish officer sailed out of the harbor in a small boat, showing a white flag of truce. He boarded the American flagship and informed the admiral that the seven heroic sailors had all been recovered and were in good condition. He warmly praised their bravery and assured the U.S. commander that they would be given considerate treatment.

Though the mission proved to be a failure, the American press extolled the exploit in glowing terms, and indeed the failure could not detract from the display of courage by Hobson and his men who had sailed the *Merrimac* directly into the jaws of the Spanish shore batteries. Each of the six crewmen received the Medal of Honor after their release in a prisoner exchange. As an officer Hobson was not eligible for the medal at that time, but in 1933 he received the award.

27

Daniel J. Daly, Pvt., USMC
Calvin P. Titus, Musician, USA
Robert H. Von Schlick, Pvt., USA

"gallantry and daring conduct"

At the turn of the century, the slumbering giant of China began to stir and grumble. The mysterious Orient had been a gold mine for European and American commerce. Russia, Germany, France, Great Britain, Holland, Portugal, Spain, Italy, Austria and the United States were all busily engaged in China trade when, in 1900, a serious rebellion broke out, led by a secret organization of radical Chinese who called themselves The Righteous Order of Harmonious Fists, or the Buddhist Patriotic League of Boxers. This colorful band of yellow-sashed terrorists vowed to destroy all "foreign devils." Their shrill war cry, "Sha! Sha!" meant, simply, "Kill!"

During the Spring of 1900, the Boxers attacked the railroad between Tientsin and Peking. Their forays began to be a source of real concern to the foreign powers and especially to the legations in those two cities. By mid-June the Boxers had the walled city of Peking fully under their control. The foreign settlements in the city were isolated. Surrounded on all sides by hostile fanatics, the legations in the heart of Peking found themselves under siege, with only some 400 legation guards to defend them.

In order to free the besieged settlements, an international expeditionary force was organized. It consisted of roughly 9,000 Japanese troops, between 2,000 and 3,000 British, 3,500 Russians, 2,000 Americans, 500 French and a handful of Germans, Austrians and Italians. The force set out from Tientsin on August 4, 1900. Their first battle took place on the 5th at Peitsang, about ten miles north of Tientsin. The Boxer forces were routed, and the expedition moved on, occasionally skirmishing and driving the disorganized Boxers before them until they reached the walls of Peking

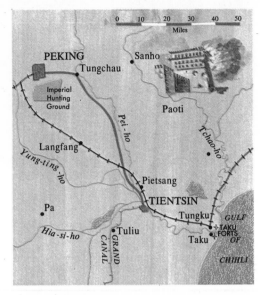

on August 13th.

All this time, the besieged legations were defended by a mere handful of seasoned troops. Among the Americans was a young Marine by the name of Daniel Joseph Daly. On July 14, 1900, when one of the defenders' hastily erected barricades was breached by the Boxers, Daly volunteered to divert the attackers while the barricade was being repaired. Alone that night, he crawled along the ancient Tartar wall to a point about a hundred yards from the defenders. All night Daly kept the Boxers at bay, picking them off with a rifle. Once he was charged by several sword-swinging Chinese who screamed their dreaded "Sha! Sha! Sha!" as they rushed at him. He bayoneted two attackers and knocked a third off the wall with the butt of his rifle. By dawn he was surrounded by the bodies of enemy Chinese — members of the Harmonious Fists who had boasted of immortality. Meanwhile the vital barricade had been repaired. Private Daly not only won the Medal

28

of Honor for his heroism in Peking, but completed a thirty-year career in the Marines during which he won a second Medal of Honor and was recommended for a third!

On the night of August 13th, when the Russian force made an unscheduled surprise attack through one of the city gates, they became the first of the allies to enter Peking, and succeeded in securing a section of the wall. For several hours after dawn of the 14th, there was intense fighting on the wall and along the streets just inside the gates. To the left of the hotly engaged Russians, the American force was busy. They did not succeed in making their way through the Tung Pien gate, but an Army musician in Company E by the name of Calvin P. Titus found a route up the sheer face of the wall, clinging to hand-and-footholds until he reached the top. There, exposed to heavy rifle fire, he shouted to members of his group below, "Up this way! We can out-flank them from here!" He waved his arms and beckoned wildly until the other Americans got the idea. Although his gesturing served to attract still heavier fire from the defending Boxers, Titus miraculously remained unscathed atop the wall while his companions climbed up to join him. The assault was highly successful. Soon the Americans were pouring shots down at the Chinese holding the gate. The Boxers retreated, the gate was breached, and the Americans were thus able to join with the Russians who badly needed re-inforcement. For his "gallant and daring conduct," Titus was awarded the Medal of Honor.

There were fifty-four other Marines and Army men who won the Medal for their exploits during the Boxer rebellion. The operation, officially known as the China Relief Expedition, was often involved in bitter fighting against overwhelmingly superior numbers of fanatical Chinese youths. In the course of the advance to Peking from Tientsin, a typical Medal-winning incident occurred. Scouting a short distance from the main force, Private Robert H. Von Schlick was attacked by a howling mob of Boxers. Though he was severely wounded, he fought on alone, killing and wounding many of the attackers. He succeeded in holding the Chinese at bay until he was rescued by men of his own outfit.

The eventual outcome of the international expedition was a success. Besieged nationals were freed in the August 1900, campaign by a unique case of international co-operation, when Russian, German, American, French, British and Japanese soldiers fought bravely side by side in a common effort to rescue their countrymen.

29

Hiram I. Bearss, Capt., USMC
David D. Porter, Capt., USMC

"distinguished public service in the presence of the enemy"

Having purchased the Philippines from Spain at the conclusion of the Spanish-American War, the United States found itself facing a native uprising. The U.S. public was very badly misinformed about the state of affairs in the Philippines. Reports from General Elwell S. Otis, who commanded the American forces in the islands, were uniformly optimistic. They failed to mention that U.S. volunteers were deserting, and that a large percentage were stricken by jungle diseases.

Many soldiers were without shoes, field guns were left behind. The average infantryman was armed with a heavy 10-pound, single-shot Springfield rifle that kicked like a mule. On half rations, the American wallowed in knee-deep mire, drenched to the skin. One report, describing these conditions, said, "... their feet becoming heavier with mud at each step, the infantry became discouraged. Some men simply cried, others slipped down in the mud and refused to rise ... Only a promise of food in the next town and the fear that if they remained behind they would be butchered by marauding bands of Insurgents forced some to their feet to struggle on."

Under such conditions, the American forces somehow managed to drive the Insurgent forces out of Luzon and several other islands, so that in 1901, the main pocket of resistance was in Samar. At the battle of Tirad Pass, Insurgent General Gregorio del Pilar was slain and his small holding force was wiped out.

In September 1901, the Americans were on Samar, preparing to make this last outpost of the Insurgents secure. Company C of the 9th Infantry was garrisoned in Balangiga. This was one of the veteran outfits that had attacked Tientsin and scaled the walls of Peking to quell the Boxer Re-

bellion. While the Americans were at breakfast on the morning of September 28th, the native chief of police knocked out one of the guards. Instantly about 200 villagers rushed upon the American camp. They slaughtered most of the Americans at their mess tables and killed the officers in their quarters. Some men who tried to escape by swimming away from the island were killed by native bolos. These were heavy, single-edged knives, a popular weapon of the Filipinos. Only a handful of the company escaped to Leyte in outrigger canoes.

This and some other last-ditch massacres carried out by Filipino guerrillas, so shocked the U.S. public, that a great clamor went up to end the Philippine war once and for all. As a result, American forces began an all-out assault to crush resistance on Samar. In the course of this campaign, in November 1901, an American force commanded by Marine Captain David Dixon Porter

landed in the Sohoton Region of Samar. Porter's second-in-command was Captain Hiram Iddings Bearss. Together, they agreed to make a surprise attack on the most formidable Insurgent stronghold in the Philippines. This fortified position, commanded by sheer cliffs, had been prepared by the natives for a last-ditch stand over a period of three years. It was located at the junction of the Cadacan and Sohoton Rivers, and was considered practically impregnable.

Undaunted, Porter and Bearss led two columns into the shadow of the cliffs. There the Americans eyed the summit with misgiving. The cliffs were of soft, volcanic stone, honeycombed with caves and natural hideouts for defenders. Near the top, over 200 feet from the riverbank, tons of rocks had been piled on crude platforms and suspended by vine cables known to the natives as *bejuco*. The defenders planned to cut the vines, cascading the rocks upon the attackers below.

But before these cliffs could be scaled, the Americans had first to rout an Insurgent force, and cross the river under fire. They attacked the natives along trails that had been lined with poisoned spears, crisscrossed with cleverly hidden pits and guarded by well-camouflaged ambuscades.

Relying on determination and surprise, they succeeded in driving the Filipinos before them. They then crossed the river, and under a hail of poisoned arrows, rifle fire and spears, the two brave officers worked swiftly. They had bamboo ladders brought out of a place of concealment in the jungle. With these they led their men up the sheer 200-foot cliffs. Although the caches of rock were sent crashing down, the ladders had been well placed in protected spots, so that few casualties resulted.

Bearss and Porter were nearing an Insurgent rallying point that in three years of warfare had never been penetrated by U.S. troops. With an exultant yell, the first Americans to reach the top charged the enemy camp. They came face to face with bolo-swinging natives who fought like cornered tigers. Fortunately for the attacking force, the number of Filipinos defending the camp was not large. After a short, vicious hand-to-hand battle, the Insurgent camp was destroyed, a powder magazine was blown up, at least 30 defenders were killed, and quantities of small arms, food and other supplies were seized.

This extraordinary exhibition of courage on the part of the two Marine captains resulted in their being awarded the Medal of Honor.

31

John H. Catherwood, Seaman, USN
Bolden R. Harrison, Seaman, USN
Fred H. McGuire, Hosp. Appr., USN
George F. Henrechon, Mach. Mate 2C, USN

". . . valiant effort under fire and in the face of great odds . . ."

After the Spanish-American War and America's subsequent war in the Philippines, William Howard Taft was sent to act as the first American governor of the islands. His policies were firm, but just, and in a few years he succeeded in establishing a democratic government and a sound judicial system in a country that had been torn by dissension and war for many years. Schools, roads and up-to-date communications were built, while the Filipinos made steady progress toward becoming a modern, self-governing nation.

In spite of these improvements, some rebel groups persisted. Outlaw bands continued to raid native settlements where the people were co-operating with U.S. authorities. The rebel complaint, as in so many underdeveloped countries before and since, was not that Americans were mistreating them, but, simply, that they were unwelcome foreigners.

One of the last strongholds of Filipino bandits was on the island of Basilan. Fierce Moro tribesmen held the village of Mundang, and on September 24, 1911, a shore party of sailors from the U.S.S. *Pampang* was assigned the task of destroying the outlaw nest.

The assault party landed without incident on the morning of September 24th, and they advanced inland toward Mundang, scouring the brush and investigating native shacks along the way. For some time they proceeded unmolested, but there was an unnatural stillness about the place that unnerved them. When they approached a cluster of nipa huts close to the trail they were following, the lieutenant in charge of the group selected a patrol to scout ahead of the main party, and he placed several other sailors in strategic positions to guard the trail. He then personally led the patrol into an open space before the native huts.

Staying close to the lieutenant was Ordinary Seaman John Hugh Catherwood. He entered the clearing without hesitation, keeping his rifle ready, and moving cautiously toward the nearest of the huts. Still there was no sign of any life, a fact that struck the Americans as odd, for in such native villages, women and children were generally busy with their chores, and dogs would bark at the approach of strangers.

Suddenly a score of Moros erupted from hiding places in and around the seemingly deserted huts. They charged the Americans, firing their guns at point-blank range. The lieutenant fell, mortally wounded. Seaman Catherwood was also struck down before he could get off a shot of his own, but although he was unable to rise, he began firing his weapon from a prone position and, crawling close to his fallen leader, he fought desperately to protect the lieutenant and to ward off the enemy attack.

Meanwhile, Seaman Bolden Reush Harrison had been standing by on the trail, a hundred yards or more to the rear. Hearing shouts and calls for help, he instantly rushed to the clearing. He was armed with

32

a double-barreled shotgun, with which he blazed away at the onrushing Moros. His prompt action felled three of the surprised enemy, who now began to falter.

The shouts and gunfire in the clearing had also alerted other members of the landing party and had brought them on the run. Machinist's Mate Second Class George Francis Henrechon, and Hospital Apprentice Fred Henry McGuire had both been stationed in the surrounding jungle, about a hundred yards from the huts. Henrechon was one of the first of the trail guards to reach the scene of the Moro attack. He immediately opened fire on the natives only to have his rifle jam after the first shot. For a second he struggled to get the weapon into operation, but finding this hopeless, he used the rifle as a club, smashed the stock over the head of one Moro, then drew his pistol and fired rapidly at the startled attackers. After a few moments the ranks of the Moros were broken and they began to fall back, with Henrechon and McGuire in pursuit. McGuire had arrived in the open area only a few seconds after Henrechon, and he had emptied a clip from his rifle into the attacking force.

Like Henrechon, McGuire then swung his empty rifle right and left, clubbing attackers as he stood over some of the fallen members of the advance patrol. In this way he fought off Moros like an enraged tiger until others of the shore party arrived. Then he went to the aid of wounded members of the party, ripping strips from his shirt for bandages. His Medal of Honor citation describes his exploit as follows: "Although himself wounded, McGuire ministered tirelessly and efficiently to those who had been struck down, thereby saving the lives of two who might otherwise have succumbed to enemy-inflicted wounds."

A fourth Medal of Honor winner in this action was Carpenter's Mate Third Class Jacob Volz. Volz had run toward the clearing the instant he heard cries and shots, and he arrived at the spot to see all of the members of the scouting party wounded and writhing on the ground, though they were still firing and attempting to fight off the attackers. Volz took cool aim and shot down several Moros, ran to the assistance of Henrechon and McGuire, and joined them in routing the remainder of the enemy.

The Basilan Island incident was the last of the really serious engagements between United States forces and native rebels in the Philippines. Although there remained some dissident elements who fought occasional guerrilla actions, organized resistance was virtually crushed.

33

Smedley D. Butler, Maj., USMC

"... bravery and forceful leadership"

While world war was brewing in Europe, the United States was proclaiming a policy of strict neutrality. But in 1914 and 1915, American armed forces found themselves embroiled in brief, though unpleasant skirmishes in their own hemisphere. In Mexico, and a few months later, in Haiti, one Marine officer achieved what is no longer possible under present regulations — two awards of the Medal of Honor. The officer was Major Smedley D. Butler.

The first incident leading to conflict occurred on April 6, 1914, at Tampico, Mexico. A boat from the U.S.S. *Dolphin* had docked, while its crew was obtaining supplies. Without explanation, Mexican soldiers arrested the Americans, ordering some of the sailors out of the boat, which was flying the American flag. Rear Admiral Mayo demanded that the Mexican General Victoriano Huerta issue a formal apology, and order a gun salute to the American flag. The demand was ignored.

When the report reached Washington, President Wilson addressed a joint session of Congress, requesting authority to use troops to force the respect of Mexican leaders.

With Congressional approval, on April 22nd, Admiral Frank Fletcher sent ashore at Vera Cruz a regiment of Marines and a battalion of seamen. At the head of a key Marine battalion was Major Butler. After capturing the customhouse, a cable station, and other waterfront facilities, the Americans advanced into the city through intense sniper fire. After three days of fighting, the city was cleared of Mexican troops. Casualties included fifteen Americans killed and about sixty wounded. Butler's citation reads, in part, "Major Butler was eminent and conspicuous in command of his battalion. He exhibited courage and skill in leading his men through the action of the 22nd and in the final occupation of the city."

Slightly more than a year later, the same Major Butler was leading hardbitten Marines against native bandits in Haiti. In this case, United States intervention was prompted by an unstable political situation in "The Black Republic," as the country was colloquially called in the United States, and by American determination to forestall any extra-hemispheric intervention by France or Germany. At the start of World War I, both of these warring nations claimed large debts from Haiti and were threatening to collect the money by force. Unwilling to see European armed forces in the Caribbean, the United States sent naval units to patrol the island.

By this time two presidents of Haiti had been murdered and others had been deposed by revolution — all in the brief period of a few months. Now, in 1915, President Vilbrun Guillaume Sam, having ordered the execution of a large number of his political enemies in prison, was himself attacked by an angry mob and killed. This was enough to bring the U.S. Marines ashore to restore order.

The Marines set up a constabulary by training 2500 natives for special police duty. This group later became commissioned officers in the Haitian army. The

Tampico

MEXICO

GULF OF MEXICO

Mexico City

Popocatépetl

Veracruz

Gulf of Campeche

Miles
0   50   100   200

Americans also built roads, railroads, a telephone system, and modern hospitals. Unfortunately, a rebellious segment of the native population resented the presence of United States troops, however well-intentioned their mission. A bloodthirsty band known as the Cacos began to raid the highways and railroads, terrorizing work gangs and sabotaging communications. After several vicious attacks, Major Butler led a force of 2,000 Marines to rid the countryside of the troublesome Cacos. A number of violent battles took place, and major engagements developed at Fort Liberté, Fort Rivière, and Fort Dipitie.

Butler's force succeeded in ambushing the Cacos leader, Charlemagne Péralte, near Grande Rivière du Nord. Commanding detachments from the Thirteenth and Fifteenth Companies of Marines, with sailors from the U.S.S. *Connecticut,* he personally led an attack against the Cacos at their last stronghold, Fort Rivière, on November 17, 1915. The Marines fanned out, then closed in on the old French fort from the south, east and west sides. Meanwhile a detachment of sailors from the *Connecticut* was sent to block a Caco retreat over a trail to the north.

On the fort's western side, Butler found a small opening in the wall. It was so nar-

row that men could pass through only in single file. Butler led a charge of the Fifteenth Company through the breach, engaged the Cacos in hand-to-hand fighting, and directed the entire operation with consummate skill. The natives fought with anything at hand — machetes, guns, clubs and rocks. They struggled until the last defender fell. Thus the bandit force was crushed and all Caco resistance on the island ended.

Shortly after this engagement, a treaty with Haiti was ratified which established a

native gendarmerie under Marine supervision, and led to a more stable political climate in the Republic. To Major Butler went his *second* Medal of Honor for heroic leadership in the campaign.

35

Ernest C. Williams, 1st Lt., USMC
Roswell Winans, 1st Sgt., USMC
Joseph A. Glowin, Cpl., USMC

". . . despite a narrow escape from death . . ."

Political corruption and civil turmoil have marked the history of the Dominican Republic for several decades. Early in the 1900's, the small nation had become heavily in debt to European investors, and when the governments of the European nations involved threatened to take action in an attempt to collect the funds owed them, Theodore Roosevelt, then President, re-affirmed and extended the Monroe Doctrine. Roosevelt reasoned that since the United States did not allow foreign countries to meddle in Latin American affairs, it was the duty of the United States to police neighboring American countries and to intervene, when necessary, for their safety. In line with this policy, President Roosevelt opened talks with the Dominican government. The President attempted to establish American fiscal controls, with the United States collecting customs and playing the role of a receiver in bankruptcy. But the U.S. Senate did not support Roosevelt. It failed to approve the plan, even though the President was already deep in negotiations with the Dominican government.

Ultimately, the United States continued to act as receiver of customs in the island. The Senate finally agreed to supervision of Dominican financial affairs until such time as all bonded foreign debt might be paid off. For a time, this agreement worked out well, but in 1915 insurrections broke out. Rebel bands became an increasing menace until, late in 1915, the rebel leader Desiderio Arias seized a fort in Santo Domingo City. With a strong force of armed rebels, Arias soon had established his own martial law in the city. When the United States offered military support to back the elected president, Jiminez, with armed force, the Dominican leader at first accepted and then backed out of the agreement.

Nevertheless, in May 1916, the American Minister W. W. Russel asked that the Navy send a task force to the area. A brigade of Marines that had been policing Haiti were ordered to board the U.S.S. *Prairie* and were brought to Santo Domingo City.

By the time the Marines arrived, Santo Domingo City was in a state of chaos, with the rebel forces and government troops battling for control. The Marines went ashore and marched immediately to the American legation while about 125 U.S. sailors occupied Fort San Geronimo and used it as a command post. As Jiminez continued to vacillate in his negotiations with the U.S. officials, the American commander, Admiral Caperton, decided to bluff the rebels. Despite the fact that his Marine units were small, he ordered Arias to surrender and disarm his insurgents or have them disarmed by force. The rebel leader was alarmed. He and his army evacuated the city on May 14th.

Additional Marines were soon brought in on the northern coast of the island. The American troops moved inland to Monte Cristi, and advanced toward Santiago. On the line of march, they came to a ridge that

had been heavily fortified by rebel forces. The Marines attacked, driving out the insurgents at bayonet point. Two pitched battles were fought on June 30th, and on July 3rd when the Marines encountered a strong rebel unit at Guayacanas. It was here that the Marines suffered their first serious casualties, with one killed and several wounded. Among the men who took part in this action were two Medal of Honor winners — Corporal Joseph Anthony Glowin and First Sergeant Roswell Winans. The U.S. commander, Colonel J. H. Pendleton, continued his advance to Santiago next day, carrying the wounded on the tops of trucks and in some commandeered cars. They proceeded to Navarrete without incident, and for a time, the country was quiet. The Dominican government sent its own troops into towns that had been evacuated by the rebels as the Marines advanced.

Although only a few rebel leaders still held out, some of these continued to put up a stubborn defense. A particularly troublesome force was in the town of San Francisco de Macoris, where a small detachment of Marines, commanded by 1st Lieutenant Ernest Calvin Williams, faced a dangerous situation. The rebel Governor Perez had gathered a sizeable army and was planning to release and arm more than a hundred criminals confined in the fort. Learning of this plan, Lieutenant Williams decided that he must at all cost seize the fort from its Dominican guards before the rebels could release the prisoners.

Meanwhile, Williams had received orders to establish martial law in the town. On the evening of November 29, 1916, he carried out an astonishingly daring coup. With only twelve men, Williams made a direct assault on the fortress gate. The fort's defenders opened fire on the little band of attackers, wounding all but four of his men before they could reach the gate. Williams and the four remaining Marines ran on. The lieutenant hurled his full weight against the door, forced the gate and advanced into the courtyard. They shot and killed two guards, forced the rest to surrender and took charge of the fort and its prisoners. For this daring maneuver, Lieutenant Williams received the Medal of Honor.

Within a few weeks, the U.S. Marines had the Dominican Republic under control. The government was stabilized and the rebels were gradually rounded up and disarmed. Yet the U.S. force continued to have skirmishes with isolated groups of insurgents until 1922. The last contingents of Marines were not withdrawn until 1924, but they left with a real sense of achievement.

37

Edward V. Rickenbacker, Capt., Air Service, USA

". . . gallantry and intrepidity above and beyond the call of duty"

Early in World War I, airplanes were used solely for observation. Few people believed that there could be any combat use for aircraft, and as General Billy Mitchell was to learn to his sorrow, the controversy over the tactical uses of military planes was to continue long after the first World War had ended. Yet it was in 1916 that the airplane began to demonstrate that the outcome of future wars would depend heavily upon which side had the most powerful air force.

In the beginning, World War I pilots limited combat activity to hurling insults — and occasionally bricks or heavy wrenches — at enemy aviators. Then a French inventor found a way of synchronizing machine guns to fire between whirling propeller blades. Soon, instead of performing comic opera acts, opposing pilots began to master the hazardous game of real aerial combat. Not only did they attack other planes, but they dived on enemy ground installations and shot up trenches or machine-gunned military vehicles moving along the roads. Thus opened the era of the flying "aces," and in the famed Hat-in-the-Ring 94th Squadron, Eddie Rickenbacker became the American ace of aces.

Rickenbacker enlisted in the army in 1917. He became a staff driver for Colonel Billy Mitchell who soon learned of Eddie's ambition to become an aviator. He had already established for himself a colorful record as an automobile racing driver in civilian life. With Mitchell's help, he transferred to the Air Service and became a pilot in France. He was gritty, was endowed with quick reflexes, and he had an uncanny ability to master the machines he piloted. In World War I, his astonishing record included nineteen decorations for bravery, while his official box score was the destruction of twenty-two German planes and four enemy balloons. After the first World War, he became a vociferous supporter of air strength. He strongly supported General Billy Mitchell in his attempts to build up a United States Air Force, and when the General failed to convince top-ranking military men, he said in 1925 that the nation would dearly pay for its blind adherence to old-fashioned concepts.

Eddie Rickenbacker was eminently qualified to know. He had already achieved a brilliant record in France when, on September 24, 1918, he became squadron commander and was promoted to captain. That night he called meetings of his pilots and mechanics. To each group he spoke for over an hour. "I want victories," he said simply. The uniform, he told them, is worthy of respect, but his men could save all the saluting for visiting officers.

"Save your engines," he warned the pilots. "Baby them along until you sail in— then open up your guns and your engines too."

The very next day, Rickenbacker set the pace for his new command. Flying over the lines east of Verdun, he sighted two German Halberstadt photographic planes; protected by a formation of five fast Fokker pursuit ships. Although he was alone, Eddie maneuvered into position for an attack.

38

First he climbed into the sun, coming in behind the enemy. Ignoring the unequal odds, he opened the throttle wide and roared in a straight dive toward the formation of Fokkers. A long burst from his machine gun tore through the German craft as it turned to escape. The enemy plane instantly went into a wild dive and crashed. The other four Fokkers·veered to right and left.

This opened a wide gap where the two observation planes were sitting ducks for Eddie Rickenbacker. Their startled observers began firing at Eddie, who dived, then roared up, attacking the underside of one of the Halberstadts. When the German swerved out of range, Rickenbacker saw tracer bullets close beside him. The second Halberstadt had moved in behind him. He dived, turned, and came head on toward the first Halberstadt.

Meanwhile the four Fokkers had reformed and were getting ready to pounce. All this time, the dogfight had been drifting southeast along the front lines into German territory.

Rickenbacker knew that his fuel supply was running out. He had to head for home if he were to get out of this alive, but he decided to make one last pass. He sideslipped his plane, putting himself on the flank of the two Halberstadts, sandwiching one of the observers between the other German plane and his own. Now he turned and sped straight in on the German's side, firing his gun as he roared in. The Halberstadt burst into flames and plunged to earth.

By this time the Fokker fighter planes were closing in on Rickenbacker like four angry hornets, but the American ace knew when to retire. He raced for his base at top speed, escaping without a scratch.

This was only one of dozens of hair-raising encounters for the "ace of aces," but it was the one that won him the Medal of Honor. The award was not made until 1931.

All during the great Meuse-Argonne offensive, Rickenbacker's Number One Spad fighter plane was the scourge of the air over France and Germany. In October 1918, he was attacked by four scarlet-nosed Fokkers of the notorious Richthofen Circus who had been following him for some time without his knowing it. Although taken completely by surprise, he still shot down two of his adversaries before escaping.

Colorful, dynamic and hard-hitting in peacetime, as well as in two World Wars, Captain Eddie Rickenbacker is one of the legendary figures of American aviation who have made the United States a top-ranking air power.

Dwite H. Schaffner, 1st Lt., USA

"...undaunted bravery, gallant soldierly conduct and leadership"

Late in September 1918, the U.S. 77th Division was advancing with huge losses against desperate German defense. The Americans, most of them green, untried troops who had never loaded a rifle or thrown a grenade in combat, were making progress in the Meuse-Argonne offensive the hard way. While the Germans burrowed into their deep, underground bunkers during nights of intensive artillery barrages, the Americans wallowed in the mud of trenches and shell craters. After thunderous nights of bombardment from opposing batteries, the weary, shell-shocked Yanks would have to make dawn attacks against rested, refreshed German troops who had not been seriously affected by the nightly shelling.

One secret of the German defenses came to light when the Americans began to capture concrete bunkers and fortified pavilions in the Argonne region. Many of the so-called pavilions were doubling as forts and rest camps for elite German divisions. They were as well equipped for rest and recreation as for war. Behind well-camouflaged facades, made to look like rustic cottages or elaborate Swiss chalets, were thick, shell-proof concrete walls. In underground rooms were luxurious accommodations which sometimes included libraries of good books, stores of vintage wines, beer and ale, fine cigars which the German troops prized so highly, good food and many delicacies to satisfy the most particular gourmet's taste. In some instances there were even halls for indoor sports, such as bowling and billiards.

Moving through thick woods against these elaborate fortifications on September 28, 1918, four infantry regiments of the 77th Division had become separated from their support forces. In charge of K Company of the 306th Infantry was Lieutenant Dwite H. Schaffner. His men, along with other scattered units, found themselves approaching the cliffs of Le Chene Tondu. To their right was La Palette Hill. Both regions were strongly fortified by the enemy.

On this day, Lieutenant Schaffner had led an attack through a veritable storm of machine-gun and artillery fire. In vicious hand-to-hand fighting, the Yanks had driven the Germans back several hundred yards and had taken the advance trenches of the Saint Hubert Pavilion. Schaffner and a hand-picked squad scoured the woods in an effort to find one isolated enemy machine gun which continued to harass the Americans.

The lieutenant and his squad crawled cautiously through the trees toward a spot where they believed the gun was located, but for a time they were unable to locate it. Schaffner directed his squad to lie flat. He moved off in another direction, but returned to his men with nothing to report. On the third foray, he found the nest. Without a

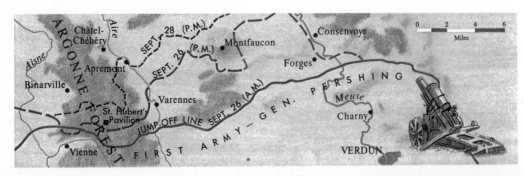

sound, Schaffner crept close to the Germans, tossed a grenade and finished off the German gun crew with a few well-aimed pistol shots. Rejoining his squad, he led them back to his company.

Suddenly there was a hail from some of Schaffner's men. He looked in the direction of the shouts to see a large group of German soldiers walking toward them with their hands held high in the air and crying *"Kamerad!"*

Having been involved in long and bitter fighting, the Americans eagerly accepted the German surrender. They lowered their rifles happily and started forward to round up the prisoners. A hidden enemy assault force instantly took advantage of the situation, attacked from two directions and mowed down most of the men in the American platoon. From his position by the captured machine-gun nest, Lieutenant Schaffner had watched the effects of this ruse with horror. Then, in rage, he drew his pistol and leaped to the parapet of the trench. In plain view of the Germans, he yelled at them and emptied his pistol into their ranks wounding several. Next, he began hurling grenades into their midst. The startled Germans, their ranks suddenly reduced by this furious one-man attack, faltered and fell back, Schaffner's anger

showed no sign of abating. Without stopping to consider that he had no support, he charged alone into one group of the enemy, lashing out at them with the butt of his pistol. He felled three or four, threw another grenade or two, killing a number of their soldiers.

Schaffner continued his frenzied forward rush and mortally wounded the German officer who had led the infamous attack. Then, seizing him by the collar, he dragged him back to the American company's trench.

"Now," said Schaffner, "How many men have you?"

The dying captain shook his head.

"Speak up!" roared Schaffner, He shook the German till he cried out in pain. Finally, in broken English, the stricken officer revealed to his captor the location of German positions, and the strength of the forces surrounding the Americans. The information proved to be invaluable. Schaffner was enabled to position his remaining men in strategic spots and hold the advance salient for five hours until relief arrived.

There were many witnesses to Schaffner's heroic exploit. The wounded men who had watched the one-man attack knew that the lieutenant's righteous anger had saved them from death or capture.

41

Charles W. Whittlesey, Maj., USA
Nelson M. Holderman, Capt., USA
George G. McMurtry, Capt., USA
Harold E. Goettler, 1st Lt., Air Service, USA
Erwin R. Bleckley, 2nd Lt., Air Service, USA

". . . with unflinching courage"

Deep in a forested area of the Argonne in France, American troops were advancing through an awesome tangle of rusty barbed wire, labyrinths of trenches, shell craters and steep ravines. This was in the autumn of 1918, and although General Pershing's grand offensive had been grinding forward successfully along most of the Meuse-Argonne front, the Argonne Forest had become a nightmarish obstacle. To the 77th Division fell the difficult task of clearing the enemy from the heavily fortified area.

On the morning of October 2nd, the First Battalion of the 308th Infantry resumed its slow advance along with other American units. They followed in the wake of a heavy artillery barrage, but the powerful enemy resistance they met seemed to have been unaffected by the shelling. Leading the First Battalion was Major Charles W. Whittlesey, a slim lawyer from New England whose steel-rimmed glasses gave him the appearance of a country schoolmaster. Supporting his attack was Captain George G. McMurtry's Second Battalion. McMurtry, another lawyer and a Harvard graduate, had been one of Colonel Theodore Roosevelt's famous Rough Riders. Between them, these two officers commanded about 800 men at the start of the attack. Both units were far under regular battalion strength. Pressing forward into a hail of machine-gun bullets and mortar shells, the two battalions headed toward a deep ravine that cut diagonally across their front. They made little headway. By noon the advance had stalled.

Despite severe casualties, their orders were clear, and after a pause for rations, they renewed the attack at 1:30 P.M. Finally Major Whittlesey's men burst through a section of barbed wire. There was a furious bayonet attack in the trenches, then the Germans withdrew, leaving a gap in their line. However, the attacking Americans were forced to pause and regroup. They took up a defensive position on the northern slope of the ravine just east of Charlevaux Mill. After McMurtry moved into the area, the two officers found that they had lost over a hundred men since early morning.

Whittlesey expected French support on his left flank, but the French had been pinned down by stubborn German defense, and they failed to close the gap. The only unit to join with the First and Second Battalions was K Company of the United States 307th Infantry, led by Captain Nelson M. Holderman. Somehow Holderman managed to bring ninety-seven men through the hostile wire on the evening of October 2nd to reach the advance force in the ravine. But during the night, the Germans had quietly filtered back into the trenches they had deserted during the American attack. As the sun glimmered dimly through a thick morning haze, Whittlesey found his position completely surrounded by enemy troops. The Germans had set up machine guns and mortars, and had poured infantry into their fortifications on all sides of the ravine.

The arrival of Holderman was the result of a major effort of the Americans to relieve Whittlesey's force. With the exception of Holderman's ninety-seven men, the attack failed utterly. In the dense October ground mist, many units lost their bearings. One company commander later described the at-

42

tack as taking place in a blank wilderness, a nightmare of white mist and deafening noise. The doughboys could not see two yards through the fog and powder smoke.

Whittlesey had been sending carrier pigeons with urgent messages, asking for ammunition, rations and support, but as each hour passed, the Germans tightened their defenses and ordered their officers to hold the salient at all cost. By October 5th the surrounded force had almost exhausted its rations and medical supplies. At least half the men were wounded. Many were dead.

Captain McMurtry was himself badly wounded, having received a piece of shrapnel in his knee. Ignoring the intense pain, he hobbled about, helping other wounded, encouraging the men and giving orders.

From the heights above the ravine, the Germans hurled a steady rain of "potato masher" grenades into the American position. To make matters worse, both French and American artillery lobbed shells into the area, in their attempts to shell the Germans. But the American pocket was so narrow that it was almost impossible for Allied gunners to bombard the Germans without having some shells explode in the midst of Whittlesey's force.

Unable to pierce the German ring, the United States commander, Major General Robert Alexander, ordered planes to drop food and medical supplies into the ravine. A number of desperate air missions were flown, without success. Even at treetop level, the pilots were unable to spot U.S. positions through the fog and smoke. Several planes were shot down in flames by German gunners. On October 5th, two American lieutenants, Pilot Harold E. Goettler and Observer Erwin R. Bleckley, took off from an advanced field and made a number of low-level passes directly over Whittlesey's position without finding it. Although German machine guns riddled the wings, Goettler returned safely to his base. There, mechanics patched up the wing fabric and Goettler and Bleckley took off for another attempt. They dived into the ravine, skimming treetops below the level of the commanding hill. Still unsure of Whittlesey's location, they nevertheless dropped supplies, medicines and bandages. All the while, German machine guns poured a deadly fire down on them from the heights above. Both the pilot and his observer were hit, but Goettler pulled up, zoomed over the ridge and headed for Allied territory. He soon came over the French lines and made a rough landing. As his DH-4 bounced to a stop, French infantrymen rushed to his aid, but the first to reach the plane shouted,

43

"*Ces aviateurs — ils sont morts!*" Both aviators were dead.

The story of a ghost plane landing in French front lines with its dead pilot and observer eventually came back to the American base. Lieutenants Goettler and Bleckley were awarded Medals of Honor posthumously.

On October 7, a captured doughboy, Private Lowell R. Hollingshead, was taken to the German Commanding Officer. Although Hollingshead was suspected of attempting an unauthorized escape from the trap in which his unit found itself, the Germans were unable to persuade him to give them information about the condition of the American force. They then asked him to carry a surrender note to Major Whittlesey. Private Hollingshead objected strenuously, but was finally persuaded to undertake the assignment, provided the note would indicate that he was doing the job unwillingly. The young soldier was taken to a point near an American outpost and released. The message he brought to Whittlesey read as follows:

To the Commanding Officer — Infantry, 77th American Division.
Sir: The bearer of this present, Private Lowell R. Hollingshead, has been taken prisoner by us. He refused the German Intelligence Officer any answer to his questions and is quite an honorable fellow, doing honor to his Fatherland in the strictest sense of the word.

He has been charged against his will, believing that he is doing wrong to his country when he carries forward this present letter to the officer in charge of the Second Battalion of the 77th Division, with the purpose to recommend this commander to surrender with his force, as it would be quite useless to resist any more, in view of present conditions.

The suffering of your wounded can be heard over here in the German lines, and we are appealing to your humane sentiments to desist. A white flag shown by one of your men will tell us that you agree with these conditions. Please treat Private Lowell R. Hollingshead as an honorable man. He is quite a soldier. We envy you.
The German Commanding Officer

Whittlesey, McMurtry and Holderman consulted together on what action to take. The temptation to accept a request so courteously phrased was very great under the circumstances. But Whittlesey's first order to his men was to remove all white airplane signal panels that had been placed on the ground in an effort to guide rescue missions like Lieutenant Goettler's. The major feared these signals might be mistaken for flags of truce.

Word of the surrender note was passed rapidly through the trenches and foxholes. The reaction of the men was instantaneous and violent. "Come and get us!" the doughboys challenged the Germans.

When the German Commander realized that his request had been rejected, he angrily ordered a direct assault on the American positions. Flame throwers were sent against the flanks. On the right flank an American machine gunner fired his Hotchkiss point-blank at the attackers, who were instantly engulfed in flames from their own exploded weapons. Beside the gunner, holding himself up with rifles for crutches, the wounded Captain Holderman fired his Colt 45. He hit five Germans before he himself received another bullet wound.

Finally, late in the day on October 7th, patrols in advance of a general American assault broke through the barbed wire surrounding Whittlesey's units, and a battalion of the 307th Infantry poured through the gap.

Of the 675 men who had first fallen into the Argonne trap, only 195 remained alive and unwounded. One of the first questions asked by the rescued men was what had become of their last carrier pigeon, named *Cher Ami*. The valiant bird had been dispatched with an important message urging

44

American artillery to cease shelling their position.

When *Cher Ami* was first released, the poor bird became confused by the deafening roar of shells and chattering machine guns. It flew off a little way and lighted in a shell-blasted tree, where it cowered and showed no sign of moving. Most of the besieged Americans watched in anguish from their foxholes for some time while bullets and shrapnel whistled on all sides of the lonely little pigeon. Finally one doughboy could stand it no longer. He crawled out of

for the bird. In later years *Cher Ami* could be seen mounted in a glass case at the Smithsonian Institution Building in Washington, D.C.

Captain McMurtry, still hobbling around on a tree-limb crutch, was the last of the wounded to leave the area. Major Whittlesey was found by the rescuing troops distributing rations to wounded men although he was himself half fainting from hunger.

After being promoted to major and lieutenant colonel respectively, McMurtry and Whittlesey both received the Medal of

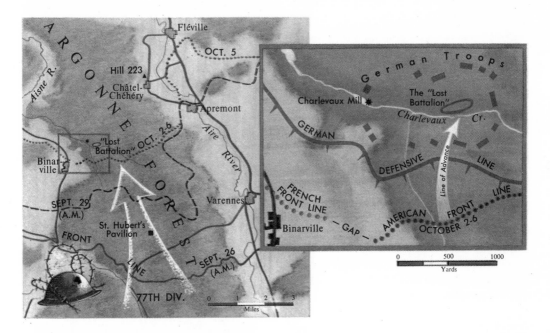

his trench and, exposing himself to the enemy fire, he climbed the tree and reached out to the perch where the bird huddled. When he managed to grasp the frightened *Cher Ami,* he stroked it for a few seconds, then tossed it gently into the air. The little pigeon fluttered upward, circled briefly over the cheering men of the Lost Battalion, then winged off through the shot and shell and disappeared toward its home base.

The pigeon arrived at Headquarters minus an eye and a leg, but the Division veterinary surgeon saved its life. Men at Division Headquarters carved a wooden leg

Honor. The Medal also went to Captain Holderman.

Thus the famed "Lost Battalion" wrote its own chapter in history, yet the popular name was the result of an exaggerated report of the event written by Damon Runyon and printed in United States newspapers. Actually the unit was not a battalion — and it was never lost. Whittlesey knew exactly where he was and kept his commander accurately informed of his position at all times. Still, by any name, the battered infantrymen who held that isolated pocket for so many days richly deserved their notoriety.

45

Alvin C. York, Cpl., USA

"fearlessly and with great daring"

The official Medal of Honor citation for the celebrated Sergeant York is notable for its brevity. It states that York, with seven men, silenced an enemy machine-gun nest and in the process captured four officers, 128 men and several guns.

Perhaps the author of the citation felt that Alvin York's story had received enough publicity without a long official description, but the incident was so remarkable that it will always bear repeating. Although he is usually referred to as Sergeant York, he was a corporal at the time of his famous exploit.

In the early morning of October 8, 1918, American forces were attacking on the east flank of the Argonne Forest near Châtel-Chéhéry. The advance of a regiment of the 82nd Division was being held up by intense and accurate machine-gun fire from the wooded slope beyond Hill 223. In this situation, Sergeant Bernard Early, a vaudeville performer in civilian life, was sent on a reconnoitering mission to test the enemy left flank. Early divided his group of sixteen men into three small squads, who fanned out silently through a wooded area and advanced to a point some 300 yards behind the German line.

Sergeant Early took the lead, moving cautiously, while Corporal Alvin York and his squad followed in the rear. Their first encounter was with a handful of Red Cross men, who immediately scurried for cover into the woods. Next, Early's forward squad came face to face with a battalion commander's staff who were enjoying a fine breakfast of steaks, bread and jam. With the exception of the major, who carried a pistol, all the Germans were unarmed. Discouraged, they promptly threw up their hands and surrendered.

But at that instant, warned by the Red Cross men, a number of machine gunners opened fire on the Yanks. Sergeant Early

fell, seriously wounded. Two corporals were hit, and six of Early's men were killed.

Corporal York now found himself in command of exactly seven able men, inside a strongly fortified enemy position. These seven men, using some of their captives as shields, backed off into the brush, leaving York to fend for himself. The Tennessee mountaineer, who had learned to shoot squirrels at a hundred yards, dived behind a tree and then had a look around. There were veritable clusters of German machine-

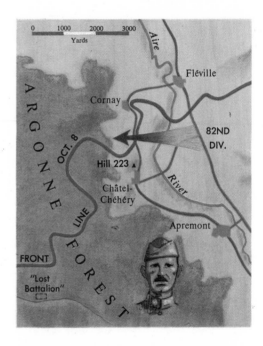

gun nests not twenty-five yards to his right. A number of these kept firing short bursts, spraying the surrounding woods and clipping the brush off so short that York was afforded a clear view of the enemy gunners. He began to pick off bucket-helmeted Germans with deadly precision. He was a superb shot, and one of his buddies who watched the performance allowed as how "he was shootin' pretty good" that day.

46

The Germans were having trouble locating the source of this devastating fire, for York's single-shot rifle reports were lost in the continuous chatter of German machine guns. It never occurred to them that the deadly rain of bullets could be the work of one man.

When at last they located the direction of the shots, an officer ordered a bayonet assault on York's position. In single file, six Germans came at the tree in a rush. York grimly picked off the rear enemy first, then the next in line, the next and the next, until only the leader, an officer, was still on his feet. By this device, York kept the forward men from realizing that the others had been hit. By now, however, York's rifle was overheated; he drew his Colt 45 and killed the German officer who was within a few feet of the tree.

Now Alvin reloaded his Enfield rifle, shot a few more machine gunners through the head, and called out to the Germans to surrender. The astounded German major, still flat on the ground with the Yanks who had taken cover, finally heard York's shouts during a brief lull in the firing. He stood up and promised to surrender his men if the corporal would just stop killing them. York demanded that the entire outfit surrender. Then the major blew a command whistle.

About thirty men emerged from their positions with their hands up. But York's keen eye spotted one who was clutching a grenade in one hand. "I had to tetch him off." York explained afterward. None of the other Germans attempted a similar ruse.

Holding a pistol at the major's head, Alvin again demanded that all remaining Germans surrender. Soon the corporal had 80 prisoners, and by the time his unhurt buddies had rejoined him, the action was all over. They directed their captives to help evacuate the wounded, then they started for the American lines. When the wily major tried to lead him into a trap, York pressed the muzzle of his pistol against the German officer's head and told him to blow his whistle. The result of the major's duplicity was simply that Corporal York collected more captives.

After he arrived safely at the American command post, he was ordered to report to Brigadier General Lindsay. The hardbitten brigadier had seen a lot of fighting in his time, and had witnessed some remarkable exploits, but he had never seen anything like this.

"Well, York," he said, "I hear you've captured the whole damned German Army."

"No, sir," replied York. "I only have a hundred and thirty-two."

47

Herman H. Hanneken, Sgt., USMC
William R. Button, Cpl., USMC

". . . unhesitatingly exposed himself to great personal danger . . ."

Following the serious uprisings and prolonged U.S. occupation of Haiti in 1915 and 1916, there was a peaceful period during which good roads, schools, hospitals and other public works were constructed, largely with funds provided by the United States, and under the supervision and direction of the U.S.-trained gendarmerie. Yet underground resistance to the new regime continued. A Caco chief by the name of Charlemagne Péralte fomented trouble in the island republic. He organized rebellious bands who engaged in acts of sabotage, forced peaceful farmers to bear arms and to take part in surprise attacks on the gendarmerie.

Finally Péralte's rebellion grew to such proportions that peasants in northern Haiti began to flee to the towns for protection. Soon this defection from the farms created serious food shortages. Native officials, in desperation, called once again for help from the United States Marines. In 1919, a Marine brigade was assigned the task of subduing the rebels. For several months, the Marines carried on an extensive campaign, yet the rebel leader, Charlemagne, continued to elude capture. He set up a well-defended headquarters in the hills and established strong outposts to guard his position. As the campaign dragged on, the U.S. Marines in Haiti became increasingly discontented. It angered them to learn that men were being returned home from France and released from service, while they slogged through an inglorious war, virtually forgotten.

At this point, one of the most remarkable individual exploits in Marine Corps history brought the Haitian campaign to an exciting culmination.

Herman Henry Hanneken, a sergeant in the Marines, sent one of his most reliable gendarmes to become a member of the Caco band, accompanied by another Haitian who had volunteered for the mission. These courageous men won the bandit chief's confidence and became officers in the rebel camp. Maintaining secret communications with these two agents, Sergeant Hanneken fed Peralte information that led him to believe he could attack the Marines with success at the village of Grande Rivière. The two spies contrived to have Péralte stay at an appointed spot to await the outcome of the battle.

On the eve of the battle, during the night of October 31, 1919, Hanneken, his second in command Corporal William R. Button, and twenty-two gendarmes disguised themselves as Cacos. Hanneken and Button smeared lamp-black on their faces. On the way to the place where they expected to find Charlemagne, they passed a number of Caco bandit units moving to the assault on Grande Rivière. One of Hanneken's agents reached him in time to advise him that the rebel chief had not gone to the appointed place, but instead had remained at his secluded headquarters at the summit of a hill several miles away. Hanneken then instructed the agent to report back to Charlemagne that a group of Cacos was on the

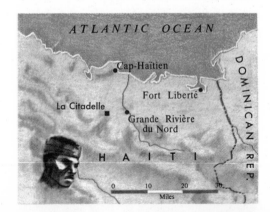

way to headquarters to report a great victory. Hearing this, Charlemagne was at first elated, but he soon appeared nervous and refused to leave his mountain hideout.

There were several well-guarded outposts to be passed before the daring infiltrators could make contact with Charlemagne Péralte. Three of the outposts were passed without much difficulty but at the fourth, a bandit guard became suspicious and drew his pistol. Hanneken, feigning weariness from the march, stumbled clumsily past the guard, but Button was seized.

"Where did you get that fine automatic rifle?" asked the rebel guard.

Button managed to pull away in the darkness, mumbling that he had captured the weapon from the Yanks. That seemed to satisfy the guard. The group then went on to the last outpost where about 200 bandits stood guard around Charlemagne's headquarters. When they reached the hilltop command post, Hanneken's agent pointed to the spot where Charlemagne stood, illuminated by a fire less than a dozen yards away. At that instant, the bandit chief was suddenly alerted. He shouted an order to his men to get their guns. Before the Cacos knew what was happening, Hanneken shot Charlemagne while Button used his automatic rifle on the guards. The surprised defenders scattered, leaving behind several dead, including their leader.

For the remainder of the night, Hanneken and his men remained on the hilltop and succeeded in fighting off a number of Caco attacks. During this time, the rebel army had made contact with the Marines and gendarmes at Grande Rivière. Since Hanneken had laid careful plans to meet this attack with strongly reinforced units, the bandit "surprise" assault was completely shattered, and the entire attacking force was demoralized.

At 9:00 on the morning of November 1st, Sergeant Hanneken, Corporal Button, and the intrepid gendarmes who had accompanied them arrived in Grande Rivière. There Hanneken reported his exploit to his superior officers.

As a result of the successful raid, Hanneken's group had routed more than a thousand outlaws, had killed the leader, Charlemagne Péralte, and had virtually shattered the entire bandit resistance movement. Tragically, Corporal Button contracted malaria and died shortly afterward, but Hanneken was elevated to the rank of second lieutenant, and eventually became a brigadier general in the Marine Corps. Both men received the Medal of Honor.

49

Charles A. Lindbergh, Capt., Air Corps Res., USA

". . . greatest individual triumph of any American"

A young airmail pilot by the name of Charles Lindbergh, better known to fellow pilots and associates as "Slim," dreamed of a non-stop flight across the Atlantic Ocean while he was flying the mail between St. Louis and Chicago in 1926. The idea was not original with Lindbergh. The Orteig prize of $25,000 had been publicly offered for the first successful New York to Paris non-stop flight, and the newspapers were filled with stories about flyers who were preparing to make the attempt. The principal difference between Lindbergh and the others lay in the fact that Lindbergh was unknown, had no wealthy backers at the start, and almost no money of his own.

There were vast differences, too, in Charles Lindbergh's concept of how the feat could be accomplished. Even such renowned aviators and aviation experts as Commander Richard E. Byrd, Capt. René Fonck, Igor Sikorsky and Tony Fokker were planning to build multi-engine planes to be flown by crews of two or more men. Lindbergh thought they were wrong. He was convinced at that stage of aviation's development, that a light, single-engine plane, flown by a lone pilot, had the best chance of making the 3500-mile flight. That way, all excess weight would be eliminated in favor of the extra fuel tanks needed to carry four to five hundred gallons of gasoline.

Once the 24-year-old pilot had the idea, he wasted no time in dreaming about it. He drew up a plan of action, then went to some of the leading St. Louis businessmen in search of money to finance the project. He told them the type of plane he needed would cost at least $10,000, and that he could contribute his own savings of $2,000. Although they were naturally cautious, the businessmen listened to him. Lindbergh's sincerity and conviction forced his listeners to take him seriously.

Not so some of the important airplane manufacturers and designers. One well-known firm refused point-blank to sell a single-engine plane for a New York-Paris flight. Another considered the idea and was willing to sell a plane to the St. Louis group, but insisted that the pilot be a renowned flyer of the manufacturer's choice.

Despite a number of similar setbacks, Lindbergh's backers, Harry Knight, a St. Louis broker, and Harold Bixby, a banker, organized a group to buy a plane.

Meanwhile, Commander Byrd, René Fonck, Lieutenant Commander Davis, and Major General Patrick all announced their intention to try for the Orteig prize. Although Lindbergh watched the newspaper reports anxiously, feeling certain that at least one of these famous flyers would be ready for the flight ahead of him, he nevertheless continued his search for a plane. He discovered a small aircraft builder in San Diego, California. Ryan Airlines was a firm of talented young men, eager to build a plane for the Atlantic flight. Like Lindbergh himself, they were comparatively unknown, but were ready to gamble their ideas and enthusiasm against more experienced men. When Lindbergh visited their small plant in February 1927, they agreed to construct the kind of plane he wanted for the price of $6,000, and they would furnish the engine and other special equipment at cost. After the firm's designer, mechanics and craftsmen discussed the technical aspects of the project, they told Lindbergh they could complete the craft by April. Thus began the first stage in a furious race against time, for sooner or later, one of the other contestants would take off for Paris. As the work progressed, Lindbergh felt more and more certain that he had put his trust in the right firm. These men were ready to try innovations. Instead

50

of brushing aside his suggestions, they allowed the young pilot to guide the aircraft's design. Whenever his requirements called for a fresh engineering approach, they came up with a workable answer.

During the weeks of construction, when he was not busy at the hangar going over blueprints or checking parts and equipment, Lindbergh was charting his route. He had virtually no knowledge of navigation, but plotted his own navigational route on a Mercator chart, following the Great Circle line from New York, across Nova Scotia and Newfoundland, then over the North Atlantic to Ireland and thence to France. In order to check his work, he read up on precise navigation at the San Diego library and determined that his plotted headings were mathematically accurate.

The Ryan Company was racing to complete the plane in sixty days. As the deadline neared, daily reports of Orteig prize contenders appeared in the papers. But disaster struck one trans-Atlantic project after another. In early April, Commander Byrd's plane crashed in a test flight. On April 24th, Clarence Chamberlin had a minor crackup in his Bellanca. Two days later, banner headlines announced the tragic news that Noel Davis and Stanton Wooster were killed when their multi-engine plane failed in a trial take-off.

The accidents were giving Lindbergh additional time, but they were not exactly reassuring. Then, while he was still making test flights in his own plane, which had been christened *Spirit of St. Louis,* the news exploded that Captain Charles Nungesser and Francois Coli had taken off from Paris for a non-stop flight to New York. This was on May 8th. With gloomy thoughts of the possible necessity of changing his plans to a Pacific flight, Lindbergh went on with his tests. On May 9th Nungesser and Coli were reported lost at sea!

On May 10th Charles Lindbergh was satisfied that the *Spirit of St. Louis* was ready. His equipment was installed, his flight plan from San Diego, California, to Long Island, N.Y., had been completed. At 3:55 P.M. he took off for St. Louis. After crossing the Rockies at night, he sped eastward to St. Louis, where he landed at 6:20 A.M. May 11th. He had made the first leg of his journey in the record time of fourteen hours and twenty-five minutes. Bixby and Knight met him excitedly at the airfield, and soon other backers arrived.

"How long are you staying, Slim?"

"We have several dinner invitations for you."

Lindbergh shook his head. He knew that 51

every hour might count in the race for the Orteig prize.

"I'll stay as long as you want me to," he told them. "But I think I ought to go right on to New York. If I don't, somebody else will beat us to the take-off."

At 8:13 A.M. May 12th, "Slim" was on his way from St. Louis to New York, where he landed at 3:31 P.M. central standard time. In the excitement and mounting tension over the New York-Paris competition, the fact that Lindbergh had just smashed all previous records for a transcontinental flight went almost unnoticed. But to serious students of aviation, Lindbergh's record time from California made him appear anything but the "flying fool" the newspaper writers were calling him.

For the next week, Lindbergh lived through a nightmare of curious crowds, irresponsible newspaper reporters and his own anxiety about the weather. A huge storm, which had centered over the Atlantic, was affecting the east coast. No plane could take off on the Paris flight, but several were poised to go at the first weather break.

Late on the night of May 19th, Lindbergh learned from the weather bureau that the storm was beginning to show signs of breaking. On the strength of this dubious information, he decided to prepare for a take-off at dawn. He went to his hotel room about midnight, hoping to get some sleep, but he was too keyed up to sleep. At 2:15 the morning of the 20th, he was up and on his way to Roosevelt Field.

The morning was foggy. A light drizzle was falling, and the field was sodden. Everything was wrong for a take-off, yet all reports indicated clearing skies over the Atlantic. Lindbergh made his decision. This was it. He had the *Spirit of St. Louis* rolled to the runway. The Wright Whirlwind engine warmed up quickly. With a nod to the men at the wheel blocks, he gave the fateful signal to start the flight.

The little *Spirit of St. Louis* gathered speed at an agonizingly slow rate. Several men pushed on the fuselage and wing struts to help it get under way. The wheels splashed through puddles. Slowly the speed increased. With 450 gallons of gasoline in the oversize tanks, the frail wings must somehow lift 5,000 pounds off the soggy ground! The slightest slip and all would end in a mass of flames.

Past the halfway mark on the runway, Lindbergh pulled back on the stick, and the wheels left the ground for an instant. He eased forward, then once again the *Spirit of St. Louis* rose a few feet. A third time, and the plane was finally airborne and rising slowly, about a thousand feet from the edge of the field. While the small crowd watched breathlessly, Lindbergh cleared the telephone wires at the far end of the field by a scant twenty feet!

The time was 7:54 A.M., May 20, 1927.

Two hours out of New York, over New England, the skies began to clear. The little plane flew on, out over the Atlantic Ocean, over Nova Scotia, the Atlantic again, and then Newfoundland. In the thirteenth hour, at dusk, Lindbergh skimmed the last hills on the eastern coast of Newfoundland and headed out into the darkness and over the vast, 2,000-mile stretch of sea he must cross to Ireland.

Sleep, his mortal enemy, pulled at his eyelids and drugged his mind. On, on into the night he flew. At times, halfway between consciousness and sleep, his thoughts wandered. But for the Lone Eagle, to sleep would mean death. He stamped his feet, flexed his muscles, pressed his face into the small window aperture to gulp great breaths of fresh air. Huge thunderheads rose in his path and he was forced to deviate from his course to fly around and between the towering storm clouds. The plane's wings iced up dangerously; he flew low into warmer air, barely skimming mountainous waves. Fog encompassed the *Spirit of St. Louis*. On, on, flying by dead reckoning — the wavering needle of a compass, and occasional glimpses of the stars.

52

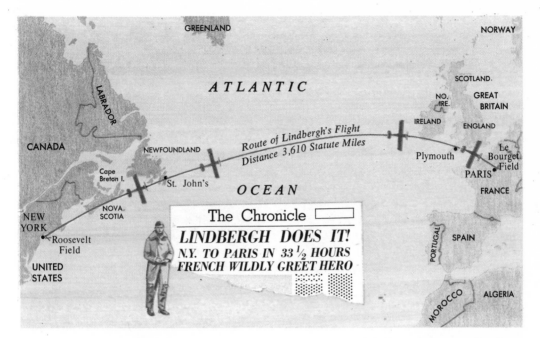

The Chronicle

LINDBERGH DOES IT!
N.Y. TO PARIS IN 33½ HOURS
FRENCH WILDLY GREET HERO

Morning dawned, the fog eventually broke up, and the sea below appeared calmer.

Half dreaming, 26½ hours from New York, Lindbergh suddenly saw a black speck on the surface of the ocean — a small boat, then several fishing boats, scattered over the sea! He dived to fifty feet, circled one boat, and when a man's face showed at a cabin porthole, he closed the throttle and shouted out the window, "Which way is Ireland?"

But the fisherman only stared, and Lindbergh started off to the east again. In the 28th hour, he came over land — Ireland! Three hours later, it was England, and finally, in the 33rd hour, France. Almost 3500 miles from New York! He had already broken the world's distance record for a non-stop airplane flight, but he still flew on toward Paris.

The sky darkened. Below were lights twinkling from villages — French villages. At 9:52 P.M. Paris time, Lindbergh faced his last, but one of his most perplexing problems. He had never seen Le Bourget Field, as it was not shown on his map. It was night, and the landmarks were all strange to him. There were the myriad lights of Paris. Beacon lights suggested that the airport was near. But what were the thousands of lights ranged along one side of the field? He circled, flew some distance farther, turned and came back. This time he could see airplane hangars. It *must* be Le Bourget. After circling the strange field several times, trying to see how to make his landing, he began his descent. He did not know where there might be tall poles or chimneys. He came in fast, touched the wheels down and rolled into blackness, expecting to crash into a ditch or some unseen object, but the plane slowed to a gentle stop. As he turned to taxi back toward the hangars, he realized that the entire field was covered with thousands of people — all running toward the *Spirit of St. Louis.*

He had made it, and all the world knew it! The thousands of lights he had seen along one side of the field were automobile headlights — cars stalled in the giant traffic jam of people coming to witness the climax of the greatest single feat in Man's history.

By special act of Congress, Charles A. Lindbergh was awarded the Medal of Honor, and the citation calls the exploit "the greatest individual triumph of any American."

William C. Mitchell, Maj. Gen., Air Corps, USA

". . . outstanding pioneer service and foresight in the field of American military aviation"

"An Act authorizing the President of the United States to award posthumously in the name of Congress a Medal of Honor to William Mitchell:

"Be it enacted by the Senate and House of Representatives of the United States of America in Congress assembled, That the President of the United States is requested to cause a gold medal to be struck, with suitable emblems, devices and inscriptions, to be presented to the late William Mitchell, formerly a colonel, United States Army, in recognition of his outstanding pioneer service and foresight in the field of American military aviation.

"Sec. 2. When the medal provided for in section 1 of this Act shall have been struck, the President shall transmit the same to William Mitchell, Junior, son of the said William Mitchell, to be presented to him in the name of the people of the United States.

"Sec. 3. A sufficient sum of money to carry this Act into effect is hereby authorized to be appropriated, out of any money in the Treasury not otherwise appropriated.

"Approved August 8, 1946. Private Law 884."

With this simple statement, the representatives of the people of the United States endeavored to make amends for the years of frustration and abuse Billy Mitchell had suffered in his valiant battle to establish American air supremacy. To understand the irony of the posthumous award, we must review Mitchell's military career from the time of the Spanish-American War.

Billy Mitchell came from Milwaukee, Wisconsin. His father had been a U.S. senator from that state. After private schools in Milwaukee, he attended Racine College and George Washington University.

Mitchell was not a flyer so much by inclination or profession, as by a desire to learn all he could about anything new, and to familiarize himself with anything he must order other soldiers to do. Having fought in the Philippines under General Arthur MacArthur, father of General Douglas MacArthur, during the first Philippine insurrection, he was a veteran infantryman years before World War I exploded in Europe. He had enlisted as a private in 1898, at the start of the Spanish-American War. Serving in the Signal Corps, he won rapid promotion. He was an indefatigable pioneer, always studying new developments and experimenting with new ideas.

News of the Wright Brothers' flight at Kitty Hawk interested Mitchell, as all new developments did. He learned to fly in 1916 when he attended Curtiss Flying School at Newport News, Va.

Although Mitchell was a captain in the Signal Corps when the first military planes were built, the machines were turned over to him because he was virtually the only officer in the Army who knew anything about flying. As a result, the U.S. Air Force had its inception as a function of the Signal Corps. In his role as Chief of the newly formed Air Corps, Mitchell talked so much about the future of airplanes he eventually persuaded members of Congress to appropriate several million dollars for establishing the Army's First Aero Squadron.

Shortly before World War I, James Martin, an inventor, came to Mitchell's Washington office with plans for a plane that could carry bombs. Mitchell listened intently to Martin's ideas, and worked closely with the inventor until the start of World War I, but he was unable to obtain sufficient funds to purchase the Martin bombers in quantity. Then, with exactly fifty-five operational airplanes, the United States entered the war. Partly because of Billy Mitchell's persuasive arguments, Congress voted one and a half billion dollars

for aircraft. In France, however, Mitchell waited in vain for the desperately needed planes to arrive. He could not imagine what was causing the delay. Meanwhile, he was in close touch with Allied air leaders. He greatly admired the chief of the British Royal Flying Corps, General Hugh M. Trenchard, whose views of the future of military aviation decidedly influenced his thinking. While he negotiated with the English, French and Italians to let him have some of their aircraft for his command, an unscrupulous group of American manufacturers and politicians were grabbing the fat aircraft appropriation and in return, building less than 200 planes of an obsolete type. These were patterned after an English design known as the DeHaviland 4. But when about 190 of these badly engineered planes reached France, Mitchell promptly gave them the more appropriate name of "flaming coffins."

It did not take German aviators long to learn that if they aimed for the gas tank just behind the pilot of a DH4, the American plane would burst into flames. To fly a DH4 in combat soon became tantamount to suicide. Back in the States, young Americans died by the dozens trying to train in these flaming coffins.

Meanwhile, James Martin, who could

have built hundreds of excellent planes for Mitchell, turned down a multi-million-dollar contract to build the infamous DH4's. As a result, he was barred from the Aircraft Trust, and received no government contracts at all.

But with his French, English and Italian planes, Mitchell, who rose to the rank of brigadier general, gathered a force of some 1500 aircraft, and launched the first mass air strike in history, wiping out a German salient at St. Mihiel. The success of this air support of ground troops was played down by the infantry and artillery officers, who would never concede that it had any important bearing on the battle's outcome. Mitchell then outguessed the Germans in a number of air encounters, and managed to shift the balance of air power from German to Allied numerical supremacy. Although the significance of Mitchell's air strategy in World War I was never recognized by the United States high command, the Germans, who had been victims of his ideas, soon began preparing to build a vast air armada.

After the First World War, the United States did nothing to develop an air force, though Mitchell continued to speak out in an attempt to arouse the General Staff, Congress, the public — or anyone who would listen. One of his primary objectives

55

was to create an air force independent of the army and navy. Naturally the army and navy leaders resented this idea and did everything in their power to block Mitchell's efforts. But Mitchell's statements were gaining public interest. He said: "If a nation ambitious for universal conquest gets off to a flying start in a war of the future, it may be able to control the world more easily than a nation has controlled a continent in the past."

Unable to win official approval of his ideas, Mitchell wrote magazine articles, books, gave newspaper interviews and made speeches concerning his theories. Among his books are *Our Air Force* (1921), *Winged Defense* (1925), and *Skyways* (1930).

American generals and admirals brushed aside his arguments and told a confused public that Mitchell was a fanatical fool. All this time, Germany and Japan listened to every statement Mitchell made and did virtually everything he advocated. They both built up awesome air armadas while America's top military and naval leaders tried to muzzle Mitchell. The American aircraft combine had acquired control of all airplane patents from World War I and continued to milk public funds while they sold their best planes to foreign powers. At Mitchell's insistence, a full scale investigation was ordered, but although Charles Evans Hughes ordered indictments and criminal prosecutions, nobody was ever brought to trial. Yet according to official records of the Senate Committee on Military Affairs, two of the companies involved in the Aircraft Trust had been financed by the Japanese banking firm of Mitsui and Company. This same banking firm was all the while working closely with the German Secret Service.

In 1921, after battling for months for permission to conduct an experiment, General Mitchell got his wish to demonstrate how a battleship could be sunk by airplanes. The experiment was conducted in July, and was observed by U.S. and foreign dignitaries. The observers watched aboard the transport *Henderson* while Mitchell's planes flew out from Langley Field and attacked some captured German war vessels off the Virginia Capes.

First, Mitchell's aviators succeeded in sinking an old German cruiser, the *Frankfort*. But when, a couple of days later, he was to attempt the sinking of the battleship *Ostfriesland,* he learned that his orders were to use bombs weighing only 200 pounds and to fly at an altitude of 10,000 feet — the maneuver to be carried out in planes that could scarcely climb to such a height, even without a bomb load. After some angry argument, he gained permission to use 600 lb. bombs. The first day of the experiment ended in failure. Next day, Mitchell disregarded his orders from the jealous high command. He loaded his planes with 2,000 lb. bombs, then told the pilots to use their own judgment about altitude.

Mitchell led the way in a two-seater DH.

Among the dignitaries on the *Henderson* was a member of the Japanese House of Peers, Hon. G. Katsuda and his staff. The Japanese watched with intense interest as, from five or six thousand feet, the first bomb dropped on the *Ostfriesland*. There was a deafening explosion and a huge geyser of water that seemed to engulf the battleship. More planes roared in, one after another, releasing their bombs. Almost at once the huge dreadnaught began to settle, then sank as Billy Mitchell dived close above the *Henderson* and waved jauntily to the awestruck dignitaries on deck.

While the pilots at Langley Field enjoyed a jubilant celebration that night, U.S. officials fumed and remained unconvinced. At the same time, English, Japanese and German dignitaries who had watched the experiment, rushed home to report to their governments that the whole strategy of warfare had been changed by Mitchell's demonstration. United States newspapers commented acidly that Billy Mitchell had

56

been "lucky" and said that the experiment proved nothing.

Under the Coolidge administration in 1925, General Mitchell was reduced in rank to his regular army grade of colonel, and the President had him assigned to Fort Sam Houston, Texas as Air Officer of the 8th Corps Area. This was a form of exile for the outspoken general, but the worried officials failed to silence him. His book, *Winged Defense,* soon appeared. It created a national furor. In it he said, "During this epoch the destinies of all people will be controlled through the air."

Mitchell's scorching fire had at last begun to spread across the nation. Speeches were made in support of his views. Political groups asked him to run for Congress. This he refused to do. Instead, he continued to state his views as a military officer, and he wrote numerous articles for magazines. When the Navy's dirigible, *Shenandoah,* crashed, Mitchell accused the Army and Navy of incompetency and criminal negligence. These accusations led to his court martial in October 1925. In this notorious trial, all proceedings were supposed to have been limited to the issue of discipline and insubordination, but Mitchell still managed to make public many unsavory facts about the War and Navy Departments. By this time, public sympathy was definitely with Billy Mitchell.

Instead of taking direct action on dismissing or acquitting Mitchell, the court martial team recommended that Mitchell be given a five-year suspension from duty and referred the matter to President Coolidge. Coolidge did nothing and Mitchell became an officer without status, as he had no command, no pay — not even an office. Finally, rather than submit to a suspension, the colonel submitted his resignation, which Coolidge promptly accepted. It was a dark day for United States air power.

As a private citizen, Billy Mitchell continued to make newspaper headlines. He warned that Pearl Harbor was vulnerable to attack. He accused the military bureaucracy of being a menace to free institutions. When Franklin Roosevelt became President, Army and Navy chiefs blocked the establishment of a Department of Air with Mitchell in command, even though the President had at first been inclined to set up such a Department.

In 1935, Mitchell testified before a House of Representatives Committee on Patents, again exposing the treasonable activities of American aircraft industries in their pooling of patents and sale of material to potential enemies, but by that time the newspapers considered the story stale and devoted little space to the proceedings. Nevertheless, he and James Martin exposed some of the most shocking facts ever to appear on the pages of United States history. Under detailed questioning, both men testified that the aircraft monopoly had depeatedly short-changed the American air force, had sold the most up-to-date material to foreign countries, and had criminally exploited funds voted by Congress. And all the while, U.S. military and naval chiefs had either ignored the situation or had actively worked to prevent strengthening of the U.S. air force.

Tired, but still fighting, America's most valiant champion of air power suffered a heart attack in January 1936. From that time his health declined until, on February 20th, he died. The infamy of Pearl Harbor came less than six years later. But the nation remembered, when it was too late, that General Billy Mitchell had devoted all his energy, had sacrificed his position, rank and prestige, had suffered every conceivable insult and degradation at the hands of the Service he loved, in his attempt to prepare America for the air age. The supreme irony lay in the fact that the same Naval chiefs who had contributed to Mitchell's downfall and who had blocked his efforts to build a powerful air arm saw a major part of their proud fleet sunk in Pearl Harbor by Japanese aircraft.

57

Christian F. Schilt, 1st Lt., USMC
Donald L. Truesdell, Cpl., USMC

". . . bravely undertook dangerous and important task . . ."

The guns of World War I had scarcely cooled when the United States became involved in a number of political hot spots around the world. Marines were still busy keeping order in Haiti. Some 4,000 Marines were in China, and in 1925 a violent civil war in Nicaragua prompted the United States to send a force of Marines and sailors ashore in that Central American country to protect American lives and property.

Nicaragua's war was between two political factions, the Liberals and the Conservatives. The latter had forced their way into power and the Liberals started a full fledged revolution. When the two opposing armies reached a stalemate, the country fell into a state of chaos, with bandits roaming the countryside, pillaging and killing almost at will.

Meanwhile Liberal forces under General José Moncada had seized several key communities in the eastern part of the country. In an effort to stabilize the Nicaraguan situation, a detachment force of 250 Marines and sailors from the *Galveston,* later relieved by Marines from the *Rochester,* established a "neutral" zone in Bluefields. While a number of United States naval vessels patrolled in Nicaraguan waters, the Marines kept open communications with remote regions, delivered emergency supplies to isolated villages and evacuated wounded natives. They also helped to organize and train a native constabulary known as "Guardia Nacional."

In March 1927, the main bodies of contending Nicaraguan armies were in position for a showdown battle eighteen miles east of Matagalpa. At this point, Henry L. Stimson was sent to Nicaragua to arrange a truce and to seek elections under United States supervision. He succeeded in drawing up an agreement calling for the disband-

ing of opposing armies, but this left the burden of policing the bandit-ridden country on the United States Marine Corps. The Second Marine Brigade was assigned this difficult task.

In December 1927, one hundred and fifty Marines and a handful of *guardias* moved against the fortified camp of Augusto Sandino, a dangerous Nicaraguan bandit. The action took place in eastern Nueva Segovia. Advancing through a rugged wilderness, they were ambushed by a powerful bandit force. A number of Marines were killed and wounded, and the expedition was forced to take refuge in the town of Quilalí. There they waited for a United States plane to evacuate the wounded. A runway was cleared by tearing down some buildings along one of the town's streets. One Marine pilot, Lieutenant Christian F. Schilt, brought his plane into the battle-torn town through a hail of hostile bullets. With many of the houses in flames, and with guns exploding on all sides, Schilt landed on the improvised runway — a short stretch of the rough, unpaved street. During the 6th, 7th and 8th of January, he managed to evacuate all the wounded to the town of Ocotal, and brought in a relief commanding officer. He landed and took off

ten times under these hazardous conditions, succeeding in saving many lives and in delivering desperately needed supplies. He was awarded the Medal of Honor.

After this battle at Quilalí, Captain R. W. Peard, who had been flown to the town by Lieutenant Schilt, took command of the Marine force and soon started out for San Albino Mines. Using this location as a base for an attack on Sandino's camp on El Chipote, Captain Peard laid plans for an offensive. Two additional units joined Peard, giving the captain a force of more than 300 Marines. On January 14, 1928, Peard's men launched an attack against the El Chipote rebel camp. With the help of a group of planes, which bombed and machine-gunned the enemy positions, the Marines and *guardias* overran a key outpost. Then began a systematic mop-up operation. The bandit force escaped and vanished into the surrounding jungles.

During the next three years United States troops continued to have skirmishes with hostile bandits in Nicaragua. The Guardia Nacional was gradually increased in strength and efficiency under the guidance of Marine officers, but it was not until 1932 that most of the United States personnel was withdrawn.

Even as late as April 1932, some Marines still saw action. On a Guardia Nacional patrol in the area of Constancia, near the Coco River in northern Nicaragua, Corporal Donald LeRoy Truesdell was acting as second in command. While the patrol advanced along a narrow trail, pursuing a bandit group, a rifle grenade fell from its carrier and struck a rock in such a way that the detonator was ignited. Seeing that there were a number of men close to the live grenade, Truesdell, who was several yards away and could easily have dived for cover, rushed for the grenade, picked it up in his right hand and started to throw it away. At that instant, the grenade exploded. It blew off his hand and inflicted multiple wounds on his body.

By absorbing most of the shock of the explosion himself, Truesdell saved several men from death or serious injury.

There were other Medal of Honor exploits in the course of the Marines' policing action in Nicaragua. Like many of America's small wars and incidents, this one is all but forgotten in the histories that tend to dwell on the much broader arenas of major wars. But to the individual soldier, a battle is a battle. The danger, the misery and the discomforts are the same whether or not the outcome will have earth-shaking consequences.

59

Gerry H. Kisters, s/Sgt., USA

". . . unhesitating willingness to sacrifice his life"

During 1942, British forces had been fighting a seesaw war in North Africa. The German and Italian armies under Field Marshal Erwin Rommel had launched a major offensive in May, captured Tobruk in Libya and then rolled for many miles in an advance toward Egypt. But by July, British resistance had stiffened. With his supply lines stretched too far, Rommel was forced to pull back his troops, and in the fall of 1942 it was General Montgomery and the British who were taking large areas of North African territory. Then, in November, came the huge Allied landing operation on the coast of Algeria and Morocco directed by Lt. Gen. Dwight D. Eisenhower. The Germans were taken by surprise.

In May 1943, the renowned German Afrika Corps was crumbling and a pursuing American unit was in high spirits. The Yank patrol was barreling along in Tunisia on a desolate road between Mateur and Ferryville throwing up a cloud of dust. The lead vehicle was a half-track under the command of a corporal by the name of Gerry Kisters. The patrol had already covered twenty-five miles that day.

But as Kisters' patrol approached a rise in the terrain, he still took the precaution of scouting ahead on foot. It was a good thing he did; for just beyond the rise, blocking the road, were two German vehicles, and off to the right of the road a battery of enemy artillery was going into action.

Corporal Kisters did not take the time to consult with other members of his patrol. He crawled toward the vehicles intending to blast them with grenades when suddenly he stumbled on two Germans in a culvert. He promptly killed one with a grenade and the other with his M-1 rifle. "I just happened to be looking right at one of them when he showed his head," he told friends later.

The next job was to knock out the artil-

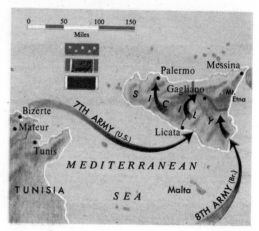

lery. Kisters crawled toward the nearest 88 and put it out of action with a grenade. As he started after the other guns, the American artillery found the range and did the job for him. By the next day, Kisters and his outfit had moved on into Bizerte. There was a lot of talk about Kisters being awarded some kind of medal — possibly a Distinguished Service Cross. This proved to be only a rumor. However, he was promoted to Staff Sergeant.

In July his unit joined the Allied sweep across Sicily. British and American troops had landed on the southeast coast of the island and from there fought their way inland despite concentrated air attacks from the German Luftwaffe. By the end of July three-quarters of the island was in Allied hands and Patton's Seventh Army was attacking eastward toward Messina.

Although there was still talk about Kisters' being awarded a medal, no official word had come. On July 31st, a detachment of nine men, commanded by Lieutenant Orsell C. Price, Jr., had been sent ahead of leading elements of their column to fill a large shell crater in the only available vehicle route through Gagliano. Once again Gerry Kisters was driving the lead vehicle in a patrol of three jeeps. When they

reached the road crater, they were suddenly pinned down by a burst of machine-gun fire. While the others dived for cover, Price and Kisters crawled up a rocky incline in an effort to locate the enemy machine-gun nest. They came upon the hostile crew so suddenly there was no chance for the Germans to defend themselves. To everyone's surprise Kisters and the lieutenant found themselves with four prisoners and a German machine gun without having fired a single shot.

There was no time to congratulate themselves. A fresh burst of machine-gun fire rattled from higher up the slope, and the two Yanks with their newly acquired prisoners plunged into the shelter of the first machine-gun nest.

"We'd better get rid of that gun, too," said Kisters. Leaving Lieutenant Price to guard their prisoners in the emplacement, he started up the slope toward the other machine gun which was sixty feet away. For a few minutes the gun was strangely silent, but rifle shots from another direction cracked the stillness. In the first ten yards, Kisters was hit three times in each leg by sniper bullets. Unable to see where the snipers were hidden, the wounded sergeant dragged himself into the shadow of some rocks. His situation appeared hopeless. He

could stay where he was and hope one of his own men would find a way to blast the snipers and the enemy machine gun; he could try to crawl back to Lieutenant Price; or, he could struggle on to the German nest. Although bleeding from six wounds, he crawled forward. Within a few feet of the machine-gun crew, he shot three Germans from behind rocks. A fourth panicked, left the nest and made a run for it.

"I've got him!" yelled Kisters. He raised his rifle and took aim. Suddenly his right arm went numb. A sniper had hit him for the seventh time.

"Hey, Lieutenant!" called Gerry hoarsely, "Get me out of here. I've been hit."

Price forced the disarmed German prisoners to climb the hill to where Kisters had fallen. Using half a tent as a stretcher, they carried the sergeant back down. Fortunately the snipers held their fire.

In January a War Department telegram summoned Kisters to Washington. There General George C. Marshall awarded him the Distinguished Service Cross for his heroism in Tunisia. This was only the beginning. He was also informed he had been commissioned a second lieutenant. And for the grand climax, President Franklin Roosevelt hung the coveted Medal of Honor around his neck.

61

Charles E. Kelly, Cpl., USA

"fighting determination and intrepidity in battle . . ."

In the darkness of a shell-battered storehouse in Altavilla, Italy, Chuck Kelly sniffed the acrid gunpowder fumes and listened uneasily to somebody moaning behind him. His senses were keenly attuned to sounds and faint shadows in the courtyard outside. He felt as though the darkness was swarming with Germans.

As the anxious night wore on, Kelly's mind reached a state of suspension between sleep and wakefulness. Sometimes he pictured himself back in the narrow alleys of Pittsburgh's north side, where he, his parents and eight brothers had lived. He remembered quitting Latimer High School at the age of 16 and going to work in a bottling plant for the sum of $18 a week. Of this $15, went to the support of his mother and eight brothers. When he joined the Army, right after Pearl Harbor, he had been itching to get into action, but he had never quite imagined what combat could be like.

In basic training at Camp Wheeler, Chuck Kelly had a penchant for tinkering with mortar shells and grenades. Disregarding regulations and safety instructions, he gave his entire company the jitters by opening up hand grenades and emptying the powder. He wanted to see exactly how they worked.

A brief tour of duty in paratrooper training at Fort Benning, Ga., ended for Kelly when he went AWOL and returned home with the story that he was on official leave. Things weren't the same at home though, and he grew restless. He returned to camp, took his court-martial punishment, and was transferred to the 36th Texas Division at Camp Edwards, Mass. This outfit, composed largely of tough, loud-talking Texans, was ready to fight the whole German Army. Kelly felt he belonged. In almost no time he made corporal, and on September 9, 1943, the 36th found itself wading into a screaming, thundering barrage of shells on Salerno

Beach, Italy. The Texas Division had its fight, but it wasn't quite the way the men wanted it. You can't smash an oncoming shell with your fist, or bayonet the man who pulls the lanyard of a howitzer when you can't even see him. The beach was in a state of chaos. Officers were yelling at their men to scatter, head inland and fend for themselves until they could regroup.

The kid from Pittsburgh stumbled into a ditch, crawled across a field and rejoined his company. German fire was still so heavy that the Americans were in danger of being wiped out. Kelly joined a patrol that man-

aged to locate and destroy a number of enemy machine-gun posts. Then he crawled, alone, through enemy territory for more than a mile in an attempt to find a U.S. battalion at a location called Hill 315. He crawled back the same way he had come, still under the muzzles of enemy guns. Asked if he had seen any troops on the hill, he replied, "Sure — but they're all German." Kelly's report probably saved his outfit from total destruction.

Later in the day Kelly assisted in another patrol which eliminated two enemy machine-gun nests. By now he had exhausted his supply of ammunition. He obtained permission to seek more at a nearby American-held storehouse. Somehow he gained entrance to the storehouse despite the fact that it was under heavy German attack at the

time. The officer in charge of the ammunition dump was glad to oblige Kelly. "Sure, Corporal, take all the ammo you want," the officer told him. "Then you can take a position at the rear of the house."

Kelly took up his post at an open window where one GI had been killed and several others wounded. He stayed there the whole night, peering into the dark alley.

When daylight crept into the battered village, the Germans opened fire again with artillery, mortars and machine guns. Kelly and the others in the house barricaded the windows with mattresses. Some of the German SS troops, after rushing across the courtyard to the very windows, sprayed the interior with bullets from their automatic guns. Kelly fired burst after burst with his BAR, until the courtyard was strewn with bodies of SS men. When his automatic rifle locked from overheating, he found another. Altogether he burned out four BAR's.

By this time the enemy troops were moving on the house in force. It appeared to be only a matter of minutes before the place would be overrun, and Corporal Kelly cast about desperately for a weapon. Then he remembered his dangerous experiments with the mechanics of hand grenades at Camp Wheeler. He seized a 60 mm. mortar shell, pulled out the safety pin, tapped the live shell gingerly on the floor to loosen the secondary pin, which he then removed with his teeth. Then he lobbed the shell into the midst of the attackers.

A deafening explosion shook the house. The Americans thought the Germans had scored a direct hit, but it was Corporal Kelly who had scored the hit. With at least five more of their number killed, the enemy soldiers momentarily withdrew. Each time they approached, Chuck threw another mortar shell out the window. Finally the United States officers decided they must evacuate the house. Kelly volunteered to stay until the rest of the men were well away. He held the Germans at bay by firing a rocket launcher from the window and then withdrew into the alley. When a number of enemy soldiers broke into the house and began to emerge into the alley through the back door, Kelly fired a final burst into the press of Germans, then dashed out of the alley to safety.

By the time Kelly rejoined his own organization his fame had spread and he had won the nickname of "Commando" Kelly. His citation for bravery, awarding him the Medal of Honor, concludes, "Corporal Kelly's fighting determination and intrepidity in battle exemplify the highest traditions of the Armed Forces of the United States." 63

Edward S. Michael, 1st Lt., Air Corps, USA

". . . above and beyond the call of duty"

The clean, soaring sweep of an airplane in peaceful flight is quickly transformed into an indescribable hell when the plane is a bomber on a heavy bombardment mission over enemy territory.

In World War II the famous thousand-bomber raids created havoc in German cities and industrial centers. Some of the scars of these devastating air attacks were still visible twenty years after the war ended. But the holocaust on the ground was matched by the horror of combat in the air. Though the "Flying Fortresses" and other heavy bombers bristled with armament, they were still vulnerable. Their formations were attacked by swarms of German fighter planes; they were forced to fly through murderous clusters of exploding anti-aircraft shells, and often on the final bombing run, when they had to keep a steady course in order to take aim on the target, they were sitting ducks for both ground and aerial fire power. The number of heroic exploits by pilots, gunners and navigators who took part in these bombing raids is incalculable. Hundreds of heroes went down in flames, the stories of their last few minutes never to be told. Others, miraculously, came through the ordeal unscathed. Not the least of the miracles was the performance of some of the planes themselves. Bombers frequently returned to their home fields with gaping holes in wings and fuselages, with engines knocked out or burning furiously. Like the bumblebee who, according to the science of aerodynamics cannot fly, but flies anyway, some of the gallant World War II bombers were shot up to a point where it seemed impossible for them to remain airborne, yet pilots succeeded in nursing them back to their bases.

Edward S. Michael, from Chicago, was a B-17 pilot on a bombing mission when his group bored through the sky heading straight for Germany on April 11, 1944. The first part of the mission was uneventful. To the right and left, the great machines droned onward, appearing invincible.

Suddenly, the first enemy fighters appeared, approaching in screaming dives from the cloud banks overhead. Intercoms in the bombers began to crackle with terse warnings and commands.

"Pilot to tail gunner — three Messerschmidts at two o'clock! Watch it! Fighters coming in from twelve o'clock high . . ."

A swarm of German fighter planes swooped at Michael's plane. Ignoring their own anti-aircraft fire, which was becoming heavy and accurate, they singled out the B-17 and concentrated their attack on it. Cannon shells exploded all over the plane, one shell bursting in the cockpit. The co-pilot gasped and slumped in his seat. Michael's right thigh was badly ripped by shrapnel, and blood saturated his uniform. Smoke was filling the cockpit, and fluid from the hydraulic controls system, which operated the flaps, landing gear and brakes, spattered the windshield.

Back in the bomb bay three cannon

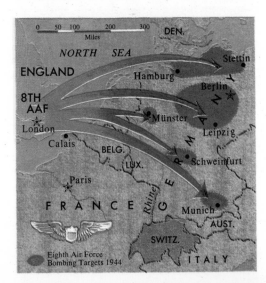

Eighth Air Force Bombing Targets 1944

shells had ignited some incendiary bombs, and the entire area was in flames. Danger of an explosion seemed imminent as the plane had a full load of incendiaries and a large quantity of gas in the tanks. At this critical juncture the emergency release lever failed to function. In a haze of pain and nausea, Michael fought to regain control of the crippled plane. Before he could level off, the bomber lost 3,000 feet.

"Pilot to crew. Pilot to crew. Everybody out!" Michael gasped the order, realizing the plane could explode any second.

Seven of the crew jumped. But when Michael craned his neck to look back into the body of the bomber he was amazed to see the bombardier still firing the navigator's gun at enemy fighters. Once again he screamed the order to bail out, but when the bombardier checked his parachute, he found it so riddled with bullets and shrapnel that it was useless. "All right. We'll try to make it down," yelled Michael.

With several enemy fighters still firing at the crippled bomber, Michael forced his craft into violent evasive maneuvers, despite its wrecked condition. At last, after being subjected to nearly an hour of continuous attack, the limping B-17 found the haven of a cloud bank. By the time Michael's plane emerged, the persistent German fighters had lost contact with him, but his gallant ship escaped one hazard only to plunge headlong into another.

A fresh barrage of flak engulfed the fiery, shattered hull, causing Michael once again to come down to treetop level. Somehow he managed to steer the bomber toward the French coast. But loss of blood had weakened him and, at last, he fainted.

Fortunately, his copilot revived sufficiently to take over what was left of the controls. The battered B-17 sputtered across the Channel. Just as an RAF field near the coast of England came into view, Michael regained consciousness. He insisted on landing the plane himself — an incredible undertaking, considering that the undercarriage was useless; the bomb bay doors were jammed open; the hydraulic system and altimeter had been shot away; there was no airspeed indicator; the ball turret was jammed with the guns pointed downward; and the flaps refused to respond. Yet, with all this, and half fainting from pain and loss of blood, Lieutenant Edward S. Michael landed his plane on English soil without mishap.

In January 1945, Michael was awarded the Medal of Honor "for conspicuous gallantry and intrepidity above and beyond the call of duty."

65

William J. O'Brien, Lt. Col., USA

". . . conspicuous gallantry and intrepidity at the risk of his life . . ."

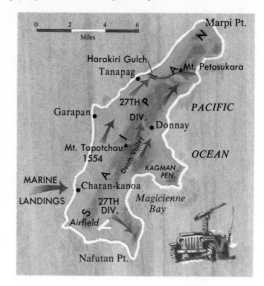

Within bombing range of Japan lie the Mariana Islands, one of the largest of which is Saipan. This island is in the southern part of the Marianas. With the development of the B-29 superfortress bomber — an aircraft with considerably greater range than the planes that had been operating in Europe, it became clear to the American high command that bases in the Central Pacific would make Japan vulnerable to air attack and would also provide staging areas for further island invasions. A plan was therefore mapped out for attacks on Saipan, Tinian and Guam in the Marianas.

On June 15, 1944, a task force of U.S. Marines and army troops landed on Saipan. The ensuing battle was a vicious one, resulting in several thousand American casualties and about 30,000 Japanese killed before the island was secured in early July. During most of this action, the Army's 27th Division was almost constantly engaged in bloody fighting. Meanwhile, Japanese naval units sent swarms of carrier-based planes into the Battle of the Philippine Sea.

On Saipan, Lieutenant Colonel William J. O'Brien directed assault elements of his unit to clear out an enemy strongpoint. His men had been advancing steadily, but on June 20th they ran into intense Japanese fire. Finding his unit stalemated, O'Brien ordered three tanks to move on ahead in an attempt to break up the enemy defense. But so heavy was the Japanese fire that the tanks kept their turrets tightly closed. As a result, they soon lost direction. For a few minutes they wandered aimlessly, obviously confused, then to the horror of the Americans they turned full circle and began firing on their own troops.

With total disregard for his safety, Colonel O'Brien ran forward in plain view of the enemy. Through a hail of Japanese bullets he dashed straight to the lead tank, leaped up onto the body of the armored monster and pounded loudly on the tank's side with the butt of his revolver. Finally he managed to attract the crew's attention.

"Turn around!" he directed them. Mounted on the tank, and fully exposed to Japanese fire, Colonel O'Brien supervised the tank assault, got the vehicles moving in the right direction, and directed the tank fire until the enemy strongpoint was destroyed. Somehow he came through this extraordinary action without being hit.

Colonel O'Brien's platoon continued to mop up enemy positions. On June 28th, he led an attack against a stubbornly defended height in the vicinity of Donnay. It was a difficult maneuver, and some of the early probing assaults failed to make any headway. Colonel O'Brien studied the terrain carefully and decided that in order to occupy the ridge it would be necessary to work out an envelopment movement with two strong combat battalions. After working out the plan of attack, he personally took command of the operation.

It soon became apparent that one of his platoons was being held up by a well-

entrenched enemy. Without hesitation, O'Brien alone crossed some twelve hundred yards of underbrush in an area thickly infested with Japanese snipers. He reached the stalled platoon unharmed, surveyed their situation and made some quick decisions. He left some troops to keep the defenders occupied, then with four picked men he led the way into a steep, narrow ravine behind the enemy position. The five Americans successfully reached a point where they could command a view of the Japanese strongpoint, and they proceeded to kill or drive off the entire force.

One result of this maneuver was the capture of five enemy machine guns and a 77 mm field piece.

With the first line of Japanese defense overrun, darkness began to fall, so Colonel O'Brien organized two platoons for night defense. In the Pacific war, it was always difficult to hold advanced positions after dark. All that night, O'Brien and his men held out against repeated Japanese attacks. In the next few days they consolidated their positions, as supporting forces moved in to occupy the area.

The American assault forces continued their difficult advance. On July 7, 1944, Colonel O'Brien's battalion held a forward position with a second battalion when the two units were viciously attacked by an overwhelming enemy force. The Japanese threw between 3,000 and 5,000 men against the American positions. Suddenly the entire sector became the scene of a wild, hand-to-hand melée. Although O'Brien's men fought fiercely, their forward positions were soon overrun by the sheer superiority of enemy numbers.

Casualties were mounting, and the Americans' ammunition was running out. It began to look as though a retreat was inevitable. Nevertheless, Colonel O'Brien never wavered in his determination to hold the position although the Japanese sent wave after wave of assault troops against the American positions.

At length, Colonel O'Brien was seriously injured but refused to let himself be evacuated. Wounded though he was, he clambered onto an armed jeep to man its .50 caliber machine gun. This he fired directly into the attacking hordes, mowing down Japanese by the score.

When Colonel O'Brien was last seen alive, he was standing upright on the jeep, firing the machine gun into a swarm of Japanese who were enveloping the vehicle.

His Medal of Honor citation concludes: "His valor was consistent with the highest traditions of the service."

67

George D. Keathley, s/Sgt., USA

"...indomitable courage and incomparable heroism"

In 1944, Allied forces were battling the Germans in mountain regions of northern Italy. Advancing through "the Boot" had been a painfully slow operation. American troops had slogged their way north through floods, mountains and seas of mud against a tough German army of nearly half a million men under the command of Field Marshal Albert Kesselring. The Allies had reached a line seventy-five miles south of Rome in November 1943, but it was not until the summer of 1944 that the Italian capital was declared an open city and was occupied by Allied forces. Even with the invasion of Normandy and the opening of a second front in France, the Germans continued to fight stubbornly along their Gothic Line in Italy.

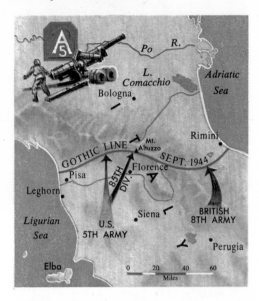

Units of the American 85th Infantry Division were engaging a strong German force on the western slopes of Mount Altuzzo in September 1944. Fighting had been extremely fierce, and the Americans had advanced within fifty yards of the high ridge when they were stopped by a concentration of enemy fire that resulted in such severe casualties that all officers and noncommissioned officers of the Second and Third Platoons in Company B had become casualties. German snipers combined accurate shooting with their unit's automatic weapons and mortar fire to stagger the American attack. In an attempt to exploit their momentary advantage, the Germans then launched a series of three desperate counterattacks. Although all three of these attacks were repulsed, the Americans had lost their initiative and seemed unable to renew the advance.

The leader of the First Platoon was a staff sergeant by the name of George D. Keathley. With the officers of other units knocked out of action, Keathley took command of the Second and Third Platoons, which by this time had been reduced to only twenty men. Not only was the personnel seriously weakened by losses, but ammunition was running very low. Keathley ordered his men to lie quietly for a few minutes. He then proceeded to crawl through intense small-arms and mortar fire, moving from one casualty to another. While he administered first aid to the wounded and spoke words of encouragement, he collected arms and ammunition from the dead and wounded men, finally crawling back to the members of his command. There he issued the weapons and the rounds of ammunition he had collected.

Keathley had completed this hazardous mission in the nick of time, for he had scarcely given out the collected arms when the Germans launched their fourth counterattack. The enemy came at the weary Americans in a furious charge made up of at least two full companies. They attacked from the front as well as from both flanks, throwing hand grenades, blazing away with automatic rifles and machine guns, while mortar units supported them.

American observers in other sectors of the line gave Company B up for lost. But Sergeant Keathley was not ready to give up without a last ditch fight. With the remnants of the three battered platoons seeking desperately for leadership, Keathley shouted orders. He exhibited such confidence and determination that his men responded with renewed courage. Groups of Germans rushed at Keathley's position in an attempt to make a breakthrough at a point which they considered to be seriously weakened. Time after time they hurled themselves at the position, only to be met with determined resistance and intense fire that shattered the attacks. The enemy suffered extremely heavy casualties during this action, and their assaults appeared to be diminishing.

Sergeant Keathley moved among his men urging them to hold on, and assuring them that the German attacks were beginning to weaken. While he was thus encouraging the platoons, an enemy hand grenade landed near him. The explosion knocked the sergeant down, and fragments of shrapnel tore his left side. For a moment, he lay stunned; his men feared he was dead.

But to the amazement of all, Keathley suddenly rose to his feet, gripping the gaping wound with his hand. As some Germans were advancing toward the position at that moment, Keathley took his hand away from his side to steady his rifle. Then he shot and killed one of the nearest of the enemy, and he continued to shout orders to his men. He pointed out where other Germans were closing in, directed the fire of the Americans, and shouted defiance at the enemy.

Although he was mortally wounded, Staff Sergeant Keathley continued to fight and to direct the action of his intrepid force for a full fifteen minutes. Some of those who witnessed his exploit believed that he could have saved his life by seeking shelter after he was hit, but he refused to desert his post. Instead, he set an example for the men and made a superhuman effort to hold the position. Even when he began to become faint from loss of blood, he continued firing his rifle with telling effect.

Finally, supporting artillery found the range and began pounding the Germans on the ridge. After a few minutes of this heavy American shelling, the enemy was forced to withdraw. Only a few moments later, Sergeant Keathley died. But the men of Company B knew that had it not been for his great courage and indomitable will to stand fast in the face of the overwhelming German counterattacks, the remnants of the three rifle platoons would undoubtedly have been annihilated.

69

Andrew Miller, s/Sgt., USA

"... gallant choice to expose himself to enemy action rather than endanger his men"

A man may press his luck just so far, and in war, any good soldier knows only too well that if he insists on taking chances time after time, sooner or later, "his number will be up."

Undoubtedly Sergeant Andrew Miller was well aware of the odds against him when he volunteered for one hazardous mission after another during the American advance into Germany in the fall of 1944. There was a grim job to be done; he was the leader of his group, and as such, he felt that it was up to him to show the way.

On November 16, 1944, Miller was in charge of a rifle squad attempting to clean out German nests in the vicinity of Woippy, France. Although American forces had been advancing steadily, German resistance was strong and dangerous pockets remained to harass the advance. Suddenly Miller's unit was pinned down by a cross fire of enemy machine guns. For a time the squad lay flat on the ground, but Miller decided something must be done to break the stalemate. After ordering his men to remain under cover, he moved forward alone toward a farm building where one of the machine guns was hidden. He cautiously reconnoitered the building, found a spot where he felt he could enter safely, and went inside. He took five Germans completely by surprise and forced them to surrender at bayonet point.

There was still another enemy gun to be accounted for. Miller took on the assignment personally. He silenced the machine gun by throwing grenades into the emplacement. As a result of his single-handed exploits, Company G moved on through Woippy and arrived at the outskirts of Metz, Germany, the next day. As the company approached the town they were alarmed by a number of heavy explosions. Shortly afterward, as they could see a number of American tanks withdrawing from the area, the men in Miller's platoon retreated to a point some distance away. But Miller himself stayed where he was. Armed with an automatic rifle, he waited for a burst of fire from a nearby German machine gun, then opened fire himself. After a few exchange bursts, Miller silenced the enemy gun. His platoon was thus given time to regroup and renew the attack, so that before long the Americans were able to enter and occupy Metz.

On November 19th, Andrew Miller was again leading an assault force against well-placed German defenses. This time he led an attack aimed at some enemy barracks. Once again he ordered his men to stay back and to cover him with their rifles while he crawled toward a barracks building. From their place of concealment, the men held their breath while they watched the sergeant approach an open window and drop inside. The building remained silent.

Miller had been lucky. He had surprised six riflemen, who threw down their weapons and surrendered. The sergeant then went back to the window and signaled his men to come on. They entered the barracks through the window, searched the rooms and took seventy-five more prisoners.

Meanwhile, Miller volunteered to take

70

three men in an attempt to capture some Gestapo officers who were preventing the surrender of German troops in an adjoining building. He and his companions had to run directly through machine-gun fire across an open space, but they reached the building safely. One of the men lifted Miller through a window. This time, as the sergeant hit the floor inside, he found himself looking into the muzzles of machine pistols pointed at him by four Gestapo agents. He talked rapidly and convincingly. Fortunately, at least one of the Germans must have understood English, or Miller's gestures were eloquent.

"This place is surrounded. You'd better drop your guns," he told them.

The Germans then surrendered.

Next morning, on November 20th, strong German forces concentrated their fire on Company G. Miller set out alone to destroy a machine gun that was becoming particularly troublesome. He ran to a house and began to climb the stairs, when he was knocked down by the explosion of a rifle grenade. He picked himself up and continued up the stairs with a bazooka. From an upper floor he discovered that the only way to get a clear shot at the enemy machine gun was from a point on the roof where, however, he would be in plain view.

He climbed out onto the roof, calmly took aim and scored a direct hit on the Germans.

By the 21st of November, Miller's unit was mopping up in Metz. In the course of this action the sergeant captured twelve more prisoners and silenced another machine-gun nest single-handed after volunteering to scout ahead of the advancing company.

Then, on November 29th, Company G climbed a hill overlooking the German town of Kerprich-Hemmersdorf. They were instantly showered by German shells and automatic weapons fire. Miller took it upon himself to end this enemy threat. He picked a squad and led them in a direct assault on the German force. Moving out ahead of his men, he walked deliberately into the mouths of the enemy guns, firing as he went. His squad valiantly moved up behind him.

Inspired by Miller's daring example, the entire platoon sprang up and swarmed toward the strong enemy position. Other platoons joined in, and after a brief, fierce battle, the German position was destroyed. But Sergeant Miller's number was up. He had been killed in the first attack which he had personally organized and led.

On September 1, 1945, Staff Sergeant Andrew Miller was awarded a posthumous Medal of Honor.

71

Henry A. Courtney, Jr., Maj., USMC Res.

"gallantly gave his life for his country"

Okinawa, the largest of the Ryukyu Islands in the Western Pacific, lies about midway between the southernmost tip of Japan and the northern tip of Formosa. Its volcanic terrain, covering only 480 square miles, extends about sixty miles in length, but is less than twenty miles across its widest sections.

Curiously, although this small piece of land in the vast Pacific seems geographically insignificant, it has been the scene of military struggles for hundreds of years. Wars with the Chinese occurred as long ago as the ninth century. There was fighting between the islanders and the Chinese invaders for generations. Then in 1609, Japanese forces conquered Okinawa, drove out the Chinese and set up their own regime, although the island was not annexed to Japan until 1879.

The American High Command had little knowledge of this remote piece of land, despite the fact that Commodore Matthew Perry had stayed there for some time in 1853. Most of the Army's information about the island terrain was gained from aerial reconnaissance photographs made prior to the landings.

In 1945, Okinawa was occupied by strong Japanese forces, and in April General Simon Bolivar Buckner led American troops in an offensive landing for the purpose of dislodging the enemy and of establishing air bases close to Japan. Buckner himself was killed in the last days of the campaign when a shell from a Japanese dual purpose gun burst close to his observation post.

The Okinawa campaign continued through June; it ended in complete defeat for the Japanese. But it was a costly victory for America. Knowing that it was one of their last and most vital defensive outposts, the Japanese poured all their resources into

the attempt to hold it. Their suicidal *kamikaze* attacks on United States naval units inflicted terrible damage, but in the Okinawa campaign alone they lost 7,800 planes.

On the main island of Okinawa, May 14, 1945, the Twenty-second Marines of the Sixth Marine Division were engaged in a violent battle with Japanese forces. They had endured a prolonged and heavy exchange of mortar, automatic weapons and artillery fire, and as night approached, the executive officer of the Second Battalion, Major Henry A. Courtney, was ordered to hold a defensive line behind Sugar Loaf Hill. The order involved digging in as dusk deepened, and holding a static position against possible infiltration and sneak attacks by the Japanese after dark. From many previous experiences, the Marines were all too familiar with the skill of the Japanese in carrying out such attacks.

For this reason, the major debated whether or not to request a change of the order and instead, to make a direct assault against the Japanese. He decided that he

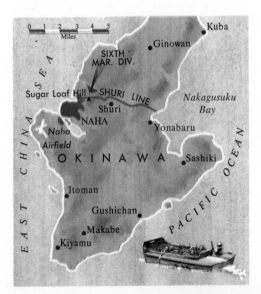

SPANISH-AMERICAN WAR, ARMY — Sgt Maj Edward L. Baker, Jr. • Pvt Dennis Bell • Pvt George Berg • Pvt Oscar Brookin • Pvt Ulysses G. Buzzard • Pvt Charles P. Cantrell • Asst Surg James Robb Church • Sgt Andrew J. Cummins • Pvt John F. De Swan • Cpl Thomas M. Doherty • Pvt Frank O. Fournia • Pvt Thomas J. Graves • 1st Lt Benjamin F. Hardaway • 1st Lt John W. Heard • Pvt William Keller • Pvt Thomas Kelly • Pvt Fitz Lee • Capt Albert L. Mills • Pvt James J. Nash •

should attack.

He obtained permission to advance in an attempt to occupy the forward slope of Sugar Loaf Hill. After he had outlined the situation and explained his plan of attack to his small force, he told the men that he intended personally to lead the way. He then started up the hill, hurling grenades into nearby caves and shooting up enemy gun positions as he advanced. Stirred by this example of raw courage, every man in the battalion followed closely, enduring a deadly concentration of enemy gunfire. They moved diagonally across the slope until they gained a position on the opposite side of the hill.

Here Courtney ordered a pause and sent a patrol to the rear for additional ammunition and re-inforcements. In a short time the patrol was back with twenty-six more men and a vehicle loaded with grenades.

Major Courtney felt that he was now in a position to storm the height, overwhelm the defenders and crush any possibility of an enemy counterattack that night. Once again he started the offensive by moving out ahead of his men and allowing them to follow his lead.

After continuing to advance relentlessly in the face of Japanese fire, he gained the crest of the hill. There, he could see that

a sizeable unit of the enemy seemed to be preparing for an attack. The Japanese force was less than 100 yards away. Without any hesitation, Courtney ordered an attack of his own. The Marines charged headlong, driving the Japanese before them and forcing them to take cover in their caves.

This accomplished, Courtney directed his men to dig in. As there was still some daylight, digging fox holes became a hazardous operation because they were subjected to heavy mortar fire. Disregarding flying shrapnel, Major Courtney moved about among the men, encouraging them and pointing out good positions for setting up a strong defense, and helping the medics to care for wounded members of his unit.

He saw that his men were well entrenched for holding the hill that night and was moving off to find cover for himself when he was killed instantly by a Japanese mortar burst.

The major's posthumous Medal of Honor citation comments, "Major Courtney, by his astute military acumen, indomitable leadership and decisive action in the face of overwhelming odds, had contributed essentially to the success of the Okinawa campaign. His great personal valor throughout sustained and enhanced the highest traditions of the United States Naval Service."

73

Clarence B. Craft, Pvt., USA

". . . utterly fearless and heroic attack"

Only a few days after the incident on Sugar Loaf Hill on Okinawa, another American attack on an enemy hill position occurred on that same island, and another Medal of Honor winner emerged after accomplishing one of the most astonishing feats of the Pacific War.

The campaign was reaching the mop-up stage, with the Japanese fighting a desperate, last ditch delaying action. Far from becoming easier, American battle victories came harder with every advance and with every attack on the well-camouflaged caves, bunkers and hillside fortifications. The key position in the entire Naha-Shuri-Yonaburu line of Japanese defense was anchored on an elevation known as Hen Hill. So strong were the enemy defenses here that United States forces were completely stalled for twelve days probing for a weak point.

Even some heavy attacks of battalion strength had been thrown back several times. American casualties were becoming serious; it was obvious that some other way than direct frontal assaults would have to be found before the Japanese could be dislodged from Hen Hill.

On May 31, 1945, a six-man patrol was sent forward to test an approach to the enemy positions. Leading the group was a rifleman from California, Private First Class Clarence Craft. They started out cautiously, crawling or crouching as they moved slowly up the slope. When they had advanced only a short distance, a burst of fire from rifles and automatic weapons, and a rain of hand grenades exploded in the midst of the patrol. Three of Craft's companions were wounded. The others lay flat on the ground, fearful of moving.

In this situation, something had to give. The remaining members of the patrol would either have to go forward or retreat. After a few minutes of inaction, Private Craft did

what appeared to be the impossible. He stood up in plain view of the enemy, and while this exposed him to hostile fire, it also made it possible for him to see the Japanese. The instant he spotted any movement on the hill ahead of him, he fired with deadly accuracy. After silencing a number of nearby enemy nests, he began to walk steadily up the hill, shooting as he went. Thus far, although he remained unscathed, he soon had killed so many Japanese that others retreated before him and ran for cover. This amazing one-man assault was succeeding against forces that had previously held an entire battalion at bay!

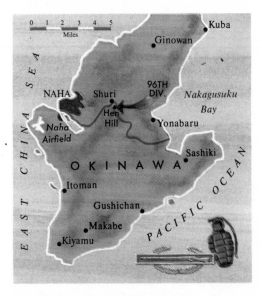

When Craft reached the top of the hill, he stood in bold silhouette against the sky, but before the Japanese were able to gun him down, he threw a number of hand grenades in quick succession, blasting several enemy fox holes at very close range.

In the meantime, because he had kept the entire enemy sector diverted, Craft's own Company G was enabled to move up the hill behind him. A few men formed a

human chain and began to pass him additional grenades so that he could continue a steady barrage against the entrenched Japanese. The line of men managed to pass two entire cases of grenades up Hen Hill, and Craft threw them with such furious speed and accuracy that he virtually wiped out the enemy force occupying a main trench near the crest, as well as several fortified positions on the reverse slope.

During the few minutes of this bombardment, Craft stood in plain view of both sides, with American and Japanese grenades sailing over his head from both directions and exploding on the slopes below his vantage point. Finally, he left the crest of the hill and made a suicidal rush at the main enemy trench. By this time, the remaining defenders were panic stricken and seemed unable to resist Craft's fantastic assault. He straddled the ditch and fired his rifle point-blank into the confused Japanese. Those he did not kill scrambled away down the length of the trench, trying to find a protected spot to make a stand. But Private Craft followed close on their heels until he almost fell over a machine-gun emplacement. The Japanese gunners were so busy firing down the slope at the other Americans that they were taken completely by surprise. Craft destroyed the nest and its

occupants with rifle fire and a grenade.

A moment later, the American company swarmed up over the crest and routed the Japanese. In the course of his attack on the trench, Craft observed that many of the retreating Japanese had taken cover in a cave at the far end of the excavation. He ran toward the cave's entrance and called to one of his comrades to get him a satchel charge of explosive. When the charge was brought to him, he threw it into the mouth of the cave. It failed to explode. Craft and his companions crouched in the trench for a few seconds, waiting. Nothing happened.

"I'm going after it," he told the others.

He ran quickly to the entrance, seized the unexploded charge, ducked back into the trench and relighted the fuse. Then he hurled the bomb into the cave again and threw himself on the floor of the trench. The satchel charge blew up, entombing the Japanese inside the cave.

During this extraordinary performance, Private Craft was credited with killing at least twenty-five of the enemy. He had, single handed, routed a strong force, opened a breach in the strong point of the Japanese defense line and enabled the rest of his company to take Hen Hill. With this key height in American hands, the rest of the enemy line quickly crumbled.

75

Don C. Faith, Lt. Col., USA

"noble self-sacrifice above and beyond the call of duty . . ."

Rated as one of the bloodiest wars in history, the Korean War of 1950–53 took a terrible toll in casualties of both fighting men, and Korean civilians. When Communist-directed troops of North Korea invaded South Korea on June 25, 1950, President Truman immediately sent United States forces to defend the invaded territory, and the United Nations voted to resist the Communist aggression.

For the first month of the war, North Koreans advanced southward while American soldiers were landing at Pusan and moving up to the battle front to stem the Communist tide. But North Korean tanks continued to roll until, on September 15th the United States 10th Corps made an amphibious landing at Inchon on the west coast of Korea. This lightning move surprised the Communists and altered the course of the war. From that time, the North Koreans began to withdraw northward. Seoul was retaken by Allied troops on September 26th, and in October, American forces crossed the 38th parallel into North Korea for the first time.

By the fall of 1950, General Douglas MacArthur, commanding the UN forces, had directed landings in North Korea, in an operation designed to cut the Communist forces in two, and to drive north to the Manchurian border. MacArthur's offensive was making such rapid progress, that Communist China sent four armies to the aid of North Korea. On November 26–27, the Chinese launched a massive assault against the Allies, tearing gaps in MacArthur's lines.

In the area of the Choshin Reservoir, a battalion of the 7th Division had taken up advance positions and was preparing to engage the enemy when they were subjected to attack by a powerful force on November 27th. The weather was intensely cold, with temperatures below zero and the ground

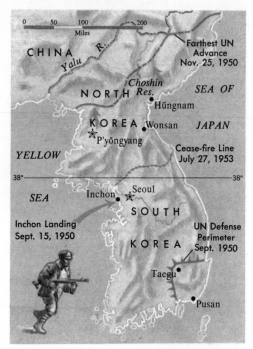

covered with ice and snow. Under these conditions, the Americans were already suffering severe hardships when the enemy offensive struck.

It was not yet clear to the Allied command that the first attacks on November 26–27 were the beginning of a general offensive, but in Colonel Faith's sector it soon became evident that the 1st Battalion was in serious trouble. Faith realized that he must take vigorous action or see his unit totally destroyed. Exposing himself to heavy enemy fire, he moved about in the forward positions, personally encouraging the men and directing the action. When Chinese and North Koreans swarmed over these forward positions, he led counterattacks, remaining in the front lines and in direct contact with enemy forces until the battalion was able to retake its former positions.

Meanwhile, Colonel Faith learned that another United States unit was operating on the other side of the reservoir. He decided

76

to join forces with them, but found that land routes were either blocked by enemy forces or by impossibly rugged terrain. He therefore reconnoitered the reservoir itself, tested the frozen surface, and decided to move his men across the ice. All during this hazardous operation, Colonel Faith directed the work including moving the wounded to safety. The last to make the crossing, he and his command passed through enemy fire to reach their objective beyond the frozen reservoir.

Faith now found himself in command of the unit he had joined, as well as of his own battalion. Without wasting time, he regrouped his forces and prepared for action.

His orders from the high command were not long in coming. He was given the mission of moving his men through heavily defended enemy territory in order to make a juncture with friendly elements to the south. Although he was physically exhausted and suffering from the intense cold, he immediately organized and launched the attack. They had not advanced far before the forward elements of his command became pinned down by enemy fire. Colonel Faith knew that any delay could be fatal, as it now appeared that they were in an isolated pocket, surrounded by major assault forces of the Red Chinese. He ran forward in the face of enemy small arms and machine-gun fire, spurred his men on, personally leading an attack that blasted a way through the solid enemy ring.

A short time afterward, Faith's men came to a hairpin curve in the road. At a strategic point, the Communists had set up a well-armed roadblock which halted the American advance. The situation was an ugly one. There was no way past this point but by a frontal attack on the roadblock. Faith considered briefly, then directed a small volunteer party to make a diversionary attack on the enemy's right flank. As soon as this assault was under way, he placed himself at the head of another attack party, and in the face of direct enemy fire from the roadblock he charged the barricade, firing his pistol and hurling grenades.

About thirty yards from the roadblock, Don Faith fell, badly wounded. After his men had carried him to a protected spot, he continued to direct the attack until the roadblock was overrun and the Americans had smashed their way through.

Not long after this, Colonel Faith died of his wounds. Yet there was no doubt in the minds of the men of his command that, but for Colonel Faith's indomitable courage, the units would not have been able to rejoin the main body of the Allied forces. 77

William E. Barber, Capt., USMC
Hector A. Cafferata, Jr., Pvt., USMC

". . . profound faith and courage, great personal valor"

Two days after the Chinese opened their vast offensive to drive American forces from North Korea, a company of the 7th Marines under the command of Captain William E. Barber, began digging in to defend a narrow, three-mile mountain pass. The position was located on a steep, frozen hillside commanding the only road from Yudam-ni to Hagaru-ri. Defense of the Taktong Pass was vitally important, as it represented a link between a force of 8,000 Marines at Yudam-ni and the main body of Allied troops endeavoring to reach the coast.

Although they were already battle weary, Barber worked his men strenuously on the afternoon of November 28, 1950. Before nightfall they had dug their trenches and foxholes and were ready to meet the expected enemy attack. After dark, the attack came with such fury that the snow-covered hill became a holocaust of exploding mortar shells, automatic weapons fire and grenades. At least a full regiment was attacking the valiant company of Marines, yet after a savage seven-hour battle, the Communists had been repulsed.

Typical of many heroic acts performed by the Marines that night, was the indomitable stand made by Private Hector A. Cafferata. When he discovered that all other members of his fire team had become casualties, he realized that he alone remained to defend a wide gap in the American lines. As the enemy assault increased in intensity, a horde of Communists came storming up the hill toward his position. With grenades and an automatic rifle, he succeeded in halting the first wave. Then, making a target of himself under devastating fire, he ran up and down the line, firing constantly, making it appear that the position was thoroughly manned. So effective was his one-man barrage that he killed fifteen of the

enemy and wounded many more before other Marines moved in to fill the gap.

The next day, when an enemy grenade landed within a few feet of the position, Cafferata rushed into a gully under heavy fire, picked up the grenade in his right hand and tossed it away before it could blast him and his comrades to bits. But the explosion severed part of a finger and seriously injured his right hand and arm.

Private Cafferata continued to fight, firing his weapon with his left hand until he was struck by a sniper's bullet and had to be evacuated for medical treatment. His Medal of Honor exploit was one of the very good reasons for the success of Captain Barber's heroic stand.

In the meantime, Barber himself was facing an agonizing decision. When he had reported he could hold the position if he was supplied by airdrops, he had received radioed orders to fight a retreating action to join forces with other units to the south. However, he knew that such a retreat would break off all contact with the 8,000 Marines trapped at Yudam-ni. It would also endanger their chances of joining another 3,000

CHINESE COMMUNIST FORCES

Choshin

Reservoir

Yudam-ni • 1ST MARINE DIV.

ELEMENTS OF 7TH DIV.

Hagaru-ri

Taktong Pass

WITHDRAWAL ROUTE

Koto-ri

0   5   10   15   Funchilin Pass
Miles

Marines at Hagaru-ri. After considering all the risks involved in various courses of action, Barber elected to fight it out in the pass, even if it meant court-martial or loss of his command for not following his orders to retreat. Among other considerations, he realized that to withdraw meant abandoning many wounded Marines who were unable to walk.

On the morning of November 29th, two relieving units were driven back in attempts to reach the isolated Company F. It was clear that Barber was now completely surrounded. During the fighting that morning, Captain Barber was seriously wounded in the leg. Nevertheless, he had himself carried through the lines on a stretcher so he could continue to direct the defense of the pass, and to inspire his men to supreme efforts in the face of overwhelming odds.

Wounded and enduring severe pain as he was, he maintained his command and held his ground for five days and six nights of raging battle. Like the celebrated Lost Battalion of World War I, this little company of Marines refused to give up despite intense suffering and what appeared to be a hopeless situation. The handful of men who could still fight not only held the hillside in subzero weather against all attacks, but in the course of doing so, killed more than 1,000 of the attackers.

Finally, Company F was relieved. The exhausted men were enabled to make their way, along with the rest of the division, to the main withdrawal operations, but only eighty-two of Barber's original 220 men were able to walk away from the bloody mountain pass.

Captain Barber's Medal of Honor citation reads, "His profound faith and courage, great personal valor and unwavering fortitude were decisive factors in the successful withdrawal of the division from the deathtrap in the Choshin Reservoir sector and reflect the highest credit upon Captain Barber, his officers and men, and the United States naval service."

The retreat of UN forces from North Korea was a bitter defeat for General MacArthur and the courageous troops who had victory almost within their grasp before the Chinese armies poured across the Yalu River. But it was acts of heroism like those of Captain Barber and Private Cafferata that saved the withdrawal from becoming a disaster. Thanks to them and hundreds like them, the Allies successfully evacuated 205,000 men by sea from northeast Korea at Hungnam. Thus they were able to resume the defense of South Korea in subsequent stages of the war.

79

John U. D. Page, Lt. Col., USA

". . . outstanding courage, unswerving devotion to duty"

Occasionally in the course of war, individuals, or groups of men, are caught in dangerous positions where they have no alternative but to fight their way out or die. Under such circumstances it is not unusual for heroes to emerge, and courageous actions are virtually thrust upon the participants. But it is not easy to explain why a man places himself in mortal danger when he could easily avoid doing so.

This was the story of Lieutenant Colonel John U. D. Page, a dedicated army man. An artillery officer, Colonel Page had been attached to the 52nd Transportation Truck Battalion in Korea, and when the Chinese offensive began to imperil U.S. forces in November 1950, he was sent from X Corps Headquarters at Hamhung with the mission of establishing traffic control along the main supply route to beleaguered forces on the Choshin Reservoir plateau. The task was a vital one, since it had become obvious that if the 1st Marine Division and the Army elements on the plateau could not be evacuated, they would be annihilated. The colonel was expected to organize an efficient supply and evacuation route, and return to his base.

This, Colonel Page could have done. But, after completing his mission, he elected to remain with the desperate forces at the Choshin Reservoir. He found that a signal station had been isolated, and he set out in a jeep to see if he could somehow aid in the unit's escape. Near a damaged bridge, the jeep was ambushed by enemy forces. Page and the jeep driver dived for cover. Finding that they were pinned down by automatic weapons fire, Page determined to rout the attackers. He crawled to a place where he could fire at the ambuscade, and in a few minutes had destroyed the enemy nest. He and the jeep driver then went on until they reached a surrounded Marine garrison at

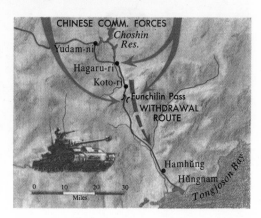

Koto-ri. Although the possibility of escape seemed hopeless, Colonel Page went to work training a reserve force of various unattached Army men who had become separated from their own units and had fallen into the trap with the Marines.

He next helped supervise the construction of an improvised airstrip in order to evacuate casualties. This landing strip was made on frozen ground outside the Koto-ri defense perimeter — a sector that was under continuous enemy attack. On two different occasions, when enemy assaults became heavy, the colonel personally directed counterattacks to clear the airstrip, exposing himself to heavy fire. Page refused to return to a safer sector. On December 3rd, he accompanied the pilot of an observation plane on a flight over enemy territory. While the plane swooped low over enemy foxholes, the colonel dropped hand grenades into the trenches and sprayed the positions with bursts from his automatic rifle.

After ten days of violent fighting, the Marine and Army units forced their way to an assigned spot at the edge of the Choshin Reservoir plateau. The first stage of the withdrawal had been completed, though at great cost in casualties. Now, however, the enemy forces were pressing their attacks on all sides, and although the Americans had

80

formed a strong fighting force by bringing the various isolated units together, they still found it necessary to fight their way free.

Colonel Page flew back to Hamhung to arrange for strong artillery support of the retreating troops. Then he returned to the beleaguered force.

When he arrived by plane at the Choshin area, he found the American column moving slowly southward, fighting every inch of the way. Along rough mountain roads, in ice, snow and bitter cold temperatures, the retreating troops were having a difficult time. Not content with helping to direct the march, Colonel Page took his place with the fighting rear guard.

When the unit Page had joined neared the entrance to narrow Funchilin Pass, it came under severe attack by enemy forces on both flanks. Mounting an abandoned tank, Colonel Page found that the machine gun still had considerable ammunition. While the attacking units concentrated their fire on him, Page crouched behind the turret and fired back, covering the passing American vehicles until the enemy attacks diminished and the last vehicle had moved into the pass.

The hazards were not ended, however. In the middle of the pass enemy troops fired down on the convoy from the heights. Colo-

nel Page took a machine gun, clambered up a precipitous slope and delivered counterfire with such telling effect that the convoy was able to advance through the pass. During the entire time, Page was exposed, but he remained at his post until the men and vehicles were clear of the ambuscade.

The convoy reached the bottom of the pass on the night of December 10th. There it was stalled by a strong enemy force that attacked from the front and from both flanks. Page knew that they were all doomed if they remained motionless in this narrow defile. He fought his way to the head of the column, then without hesitation, he ran headlong into the thick of the enemy attack force, firing his weapon as he went. The sheer audacity of this one-man attack stunned the enemy and so surprised them that they became confused, fell back in disorder and endured heavy casualties. Without regard to his own safety, the colonel remained in front of his companions, urging them to keep pressing forward. Page continued to fire and to fight singlehanded, sometimes engaging the enemy in hand-to-hand combat.

Finally the inevitable happened. John Page was mortally wounded, and he fell in the midst of the enemy force he had succeeded in breaking up.

81

Roger H. C. Donlon, Capt., USA

". . . extraordinary heroism and intrepidity at the risk of his own life . . ."

Some months before the major buildup of U.S. forces in Vietnam, American military personnel were limited primarily to air observation and to advisory roles with the Vietnamese army. The American public had little concept of what these advisers were actually doing. Newspaper reports gave few details. Sometimes casualties were mentioned, but in general, the impression in the United States was that American officers and men were merely helping to train and advise the native troops.

In July 1964, one American team of "advisers" was working with a force of 311 Vietnamese in an area close to the borders of Laos and North Vietnam. Their Camp Nam Dong had been fortified for defense of the area, with barbed wire around outer and inner perimeters and five mortar pits placed at strategic points of the inner circle. Their largest weapons were 81 mm mortars. These were placed in the centers of circular pits about four feet deep and about the area of an average room. Sandbags were piled around the rims for added protection. A concrete bunker had been built at the rear of each pit to house ammunition.

The camp had been established in a section that had been heavily infiltrated by Communist guerrillas. In the valley guarded by Camp Nam Dong were nine villages with a total population of approximately 5,000.

Commanding the American team was Captain Roger Donlon, a career officer whose home town was Saugerties, N.Y. During five weeks of military inactivity, the Americans had served the nearby communities by digging wells, helping to build schools, and aiding any natives who were ill. In addition to Captain Donlon, there were eleven other U.S. army men, including two medical corpsmen, Sergeant Thomas L. Gregg and Sergeant Terrance D. Terrin, and an Australian warrant officer by the

name of Kevin Conway.

After a tense 4th of July weekend, the American team in Camp Nam Dong was expecting trouble. The native villagers had been unnaturally quiet and nervous and Donlon's team were convinced that a Communist Viet Cong attack was imminent. Two separate patrols were sent out but turned up little information except the grim evidence of the murder of two village chiefs. No one could or would tell anything about the circumstances surrounding either of these murders.

A little after 2:00 A.M. Monday morning, July 6th, without warning, the attack came. Captain Donlon had been making a routine inspection of the camp's defenses, and had started to open the screen door to the mess hall when a roaring blast and the flash of an explosion knocked him backward. He rushed at once to the Command Post next door as mortar shells and hand grenades began to explode all over the camp. At the Command Post Sergeant Gabriel Alamo was talking excitedly on the telephone to Sergeant Keith Daniels, who was on duty in the communications room. Daniels had just time to radio Da Nang for a flare ship and an air strike on the Viet Cong attackers before he heard a series of shell bursts "walking" toward the building. He literally dived out the door seconds before the communications room was blown to bits.

With automatic weapons spitting death from all directions and with shells bursting everywhere, Donlon and Alamo dragged ammunition and equipment from the burning buildings. Then Donlon raced off to see how his men were doing. He sprinted across the compound, trying to dodge mortar bursts. At one point he was knocked down by the concussion of an exploding shell. Shaken and minus one shoe, he scrambled

82

into a nearby mortar pit. There he found Sergeant Merwin Woods firing the mortar shells with astonishing rapidity, alternating illuminating shells with high explosives. It was essential to illuminate the dark areas beyond the barbed wire, where hundreds of the enemy were advancing on the camp. In the eerie light of star shells, they saw that some Viet Cong guerrillas had penetrated the outer perimeter area.

Sergeant John Houston, firing his automatic rifle, yelled to Donlon, "They're over here!" The captain started toward him when a mortar shell bowled Donlon over. This time he lost his pistol belt and his other shoe. Crawling into another mortar pit, he perceived by the light of an illumination shell that three V.C.'s (Viet Cong) were crouching by the gate. Some bursts from his AR-15 dispatched them. It was found later that the V.C.'s, one a captain, had been carrying demolition equipment.

By this time Donlon's arm was bleeding, his stocking-covered feet were torn by rocks, his face was cut, and he had a shrapnel wound in his stomach.

All this time Sergeant Houston continued to run back and forth along an earth barricade, firing his weapon from different positions. Sergeant Terrin had been trying to help Houston by firing steadily at the enemy positions in front of the earth barricade. The V.C.'s were thus kept pinned down, hiding among some ammunition bunkers, some distance away, and none had succeeded in advancing any closer. Suddenly Houston slumped forward on the mound and lay still. The Viet Cong began to move closer to the earthworks where Houston had fallen. Terrin left his own cover in an attempt to help Houston, but he had gone only a few feet when his automatic rifle was blasted out of his hand by V.C. fire.

Donlon could see Terrin standing silhouetted against the light of exploding shells. His hand and arm were bleeding badly, and he seemed dazed. When the captain yelled at him to take cover, Terrin joined a Vietnamese group and continued to fight with one arm, firing Houston's AR-15 from his hip. His left arm hung uselessly at his side. Whenever he paused to throw a grenade, he pulled out the pin with his teeth.

The Viet Cong had now completely overrun the outer perimeter. Donlon, conscious only of the noise and confusion about him and the pain of his aching feet, shouted to Terrin and ordered him to look after Houston. Terrin and a Nung carried the sergeant to the protection of a deep entrenchment but Sergeant Houston was dead.

83

Meanwhile, Staff Sergeant Daniels had joined a group of "Nungs" (Vietnamese of Chinese extraction) who were operating a machine gun near the south end of the camp. He stayed with them for a time, then ran toward a central point where he could get a good position to fire at the enemy. He was knocked down by an explosion, found Sergeant 1/c Thurman R. Brown's mortar pit and rushed down the steps into it. At that moment the V.C.'s began to climb the barbed wire fence. A large group of the enemy appeared to be preparing for a charge. There were at least a hundred men creeping through tall grass. When several of them rose and ran toward the bunker with a shout, Daniels fired a long burst from his AR-15. A moment later Gregg joined them in the pit. Between them, they managed to cut down the first wave of the attack.

Donlon had been working his way across the camp in search of the medic, Gregg. He ran, crouching, ducking behind every possible protective cover and finally was directed to Brown's pit by the shouts of its occupants. The captain directed Gregg to look after the wounded.

"You all right, sir?" asked Gregg.

Donlon, although battered and bleeding himself, sent Gregg off to look after the others. In vain, he looked and waited for some sign of air support. Next he left Brown's pit and ran some forty yards in an attempt to reach Sergeant 1/c Vernon Beeson's mortar pit. On the way he stepped on a nail in a strip of plywood. He reached down, ripped the nail out of his foot, and finding himself pinned down by enemy automatic rifle fire, hobbled back to Brown's position. Gregg soon appeared with much needed bandages.

"You're wounded," he told Donlon. "Let me patch you up."

Again Donlon shook off the medic and ordered him to tend to the others while he himself continued on his rounds. As he passed the ammunition supply room, it blew up. The concussion knocked him down again. His left leg was ripped by shrapnel, but he crawled on to Sergeant Mike Disser's pit.

By now the Viet Cong had broken through the outer perimeter, and what appeared to be hundreds of them were swarming into the area between the outer perimeter and the inner barbed wire fence. This brought them close enough to throw grenades. Disser was working his 60 mm mortar without a pause. At the forward edge of the pit, Sergeant Alamo was firing an automatic rifle, while Lieutenant Jay Olejniczac covered the left flank with an AR-15 and a grenade launcher.

Disser suddenly interrupted his mortar activity, picked up an automatic rifle and blasted away at a point right over their heads. A Viet Cong attacker was on the parapet, preparing to toss a grenade into the pit. As he fell backward, his grenade dropped to the floor of the pit, but it failed to explode. Now other enemy hand grenades began to land in the pit. The men dived for cover and survived the first few explosions. Had they been the more powerful American grenades, all in the pit would have been killed. V.C. grenades did less damage. However, Lieutenant Olejniczac's foot was injured and Sergeant Disser's foot and lower leg were bleeding. Sergeant Alamo was badly hurt.

Finally even the Viet Cong "duds" were too much for them, and Donlon ordered everybody out of the pit. While he kept up a steady fire with his automatic rifle, the others withdrew to a nearby ditch. Donlon started to leave also but seeing Alamo sitting dazed on the steps of the pit, he lifted the sergeant bodily and started up the steps when the blast of a mortar shell lifted him completely off his feet and sent him sprawling. He fell back inside the bunker and lost consciousness.

When he came to, his shoulder was covered with blood. There was nothing further he could do for Alamo; the sergeant was dead. So Donlon picked up the 60 mm mortar, carried it some thirty yards to a pile of cinder blocks which, he felt, would offer some protection. There he found four wounded "Nungs", and he took time out to bandage them with strips torn from his own T shirt. Then he encouraged the Nungs to go on fighting. He made three more trips back to the abandoned mortar pit, clearing out all ammunition and weapons in order to keep them out of the hands of infiltrating Viet Cong.

On his way back from the third visit to the pit, a flying piece of shrapnel bit into Donlon's left leg. Still, he somehow made it

to Sergeant Woods' mortar pit. There he helped direct the mortar fire to spots where he had observed enemy movement. By now his injured feet were bleeding profusely. He set out to find some shoes, but a mortar blast knocked him down. Slightly dazed, he crawled to a place where Disser and Jay had taken up a position in a trench. Gregg caught up with him, and again asked Donlon to let him treat his wounds. Again Donlon refused.

Finally, at 4:04 A.M., a flare ship arrived and dropped flares to light up the perimeter. The presence of a friendly plane gave the camp fresh hope, though there was still no sign of an air strike from Da Nang.

When a Viet Cong loudspeaker, broadcasting propaganda, urged the Vietnamese to surrender or be slaughtered, the entire camp fell silent. The raucous voice seemed to have cast a spell over the native troops. In any case they momentarily withheld their fire and listened to the loudspeaker. Donlon suggested that Sergeant Brown lob some mortar shells in the direction of the voice. After a few rounds, the loudspeaker fell silent, and the camp defenders went into action again.

Seeing Captain Donlon's condition in the faint light of dawn, Sergeant Beeson insisted he sit down. Beeson bandaged the worst of Donlon's wounds; then the captain moved on to check up on the aid stations. He made it to the Command Post set up behind a wall of cinder blocks, although once more he was knocked off his feet by an exploding grenade. From the C.P., he observed some Viet Cong behind tree stumps some fifty yards distant. The V.C.'s were throwing grenades in clusters. Donlon shouted to Woods to try lobbing a mortar shell on them, even though the range was too close for normal mortar fire. With his mortar pointed almost straight up, Woods found the range, blew the tree stumps to bits and ended the last Viet Cong assault on the perimeter.

Roger Donlon was awarded the Medal of Honor by President Lyndon Johnson in a White House ceremony on December 5, 1964.

While Donlon accepted the honor proudly, he insisted that the Medal belonged equally to all the men of his Special Forces Group. "I solemnly pledge," he said, "that whatever good flows from it for me will be passed on, intact, to the valiant men of my team, Detachment A-726 of the 7th Special Forces Group."

Adapted from OUTPOST OF FREEDOM by Captain Roger H. C. Donlon as told to Warren Rogers. Reprinted with the permission of McGraw-Hill Book Company. Copyright © 1965 by Roger Donlon & Warren Rogers.

85

Medal of Honor Oddities

"Gallant and meritorious service in carrying the colors . . ."

During the Civil War, and for some years afterward when the Army was fighting Indians on the western plains, the Medal of Honor was often awarded for deeds that would now be considered more melodramatic than heroic. In some cases, citations were later stricken from the roll after regulations for the Award were tightened. But in reviewing some of the past records, it becomes clear that popular notions of valor have changed to some degree with the changing times. War has lost its oldtime aura of glamor. An act which was once considered heroic might now be looked upon as merely foolhardy. Modern warfare is seen as a strictly practical, if ugly and unpleasant, job to be done. Because it is a mortally dangerous job, the men who see it through are the heroes.

The situation was different in the nineteenth century. Then the cavalry, on spirited horses, still made daring charges; and the standard bearers, whether mounted or on foot, carried the colors high, even in the sound and fury of violent battle. This matter of carrying the flag into battle became the subject of a surprising number of Medal of Honor awards during the Civil War. One citation after another reads simply, "Capture of flag." Evidently no other words describing these exploits were considered necessary. It was enough that a man had risked death to capture the enemy colors to the glory of his country.

The Civil War had scarcely begun when, on May 24, 1861, the Eleventh New York Fire Zouaves marched into Alexandria, Virginia, to man Union defenses south of Washington. As the Zouaves advanced down the street, a Confederate flag was raised to the top of a flagpole on the roof of a hotel known as the Marshall House. The Union commander, Colonel Ephraim E. Ellsworth, halted his column, jumped from his horse and rushed to the hotel entrance, followed by Private Francis E. Brownell. A moment later, Ellsworth appeared on the Marshall House roof. He hauled down the rebel flag, then brought it to the street where he was greeted by the lusty cheers of his men. At that moment a shot rang out. Colonel Ellsworth fell dead at the foot of the hotel steps. Instantly, Private Brownell whirled, fired at the assassin, then ran forward and thrust his bayonet into the fallen rebel — a man named Jackson. After the war, Brownell was awarded the Medal of Honor for this deed.

Many stories have been told of gallant cavalry charges and of planting the colors on captured enemy fortifications. One such daring exploit won Colonel Galusha Pennypacker a Medal of Honor. Pennypacker, who was promoted to Major General during the Civil War, yet had barely reached age 21 as the war ended, led an attack on Fort Fisher, North Carolina. So heavy was the Confederate fire from the fort, that his brigade began to fall back. Pennypacker seized the standard of the 97th Pennsylvania, spurred his horse forward, and waving the flag with one hand, he called to his men to follow him. He then galloped up a slope of the fortifications, and planted the flag at the top, while the men of his regiment cheered and charged up the slope behind him. An instant after he had planted the flag, a minie ball struck Pennypacker, fracturing his pelvic bone. He was thought to be dead, but later revived and continued in active duty with the Army until 1883.

Among the Civil War's many flag incidents was one that is particularly noteworthy because of the later fame of the hero involved. At Missionary Ridge, Tennessee, in November 1863, First Lieutenant Arthur MacArthur, Jr. was credited with seizing the colors of his regiment during a crucial

86

period of the battle. He carried the flag forward through a storm of enemy fire, and planted it on the fortifications at the crest of Missionary Ridge.

For this display of courage in the face of the enemy, Arthur MacArthur was awarded the Medal of Honor though the actual issue of the Medal was not made until 1890. Arthur MacArthur's importance as a military leader grew as time went on. He became military governor of the Philippines in 1900. As a lieutenant general he served as Assistant Chief of Staff of the U.S. Army in 1906. He retired in 1909.

His famous son, Douglas MacArthur, was also a Medal of Honor winner. He became the symbol of American determination to return to the Philippines after their seizure by Japanese forces in World War II.

Thus, both father and son were famous generals, both served in the Philippines, and both were awarded the coveted Medal of Honor.

Probably the youngest Medal of Honor recipients were two boys of 15 who served in the Civil War. One was J. C. Julius Langbein, a drummer boy. Like many other youngsters who became drummers for the Army in those days, he frequently played stirring drum rolls for his regiment during battles, exposing himself to enemy fire without a weapon of his own to defend himself. Yet young Langbein was the victim of jokes aimed at him by older troopers who would never let him forget his tender age. One sergeant by the name of Mossman was constantly making fun of him. In an engagement at Camden, North Carolina, April 19, 1862, Julius drummed smartly for a charge that was soon broken up by intense Confederate fire. Sergeant Mossman received a head wound and began to wander aimlessly across a field, directly in the line of fire. Without hesitation, Langbein ran to the dazed sergeant and led him to safety. At a field hospital tent, the surgeon decided that Mossman was nearly dead and would not treat him. As the Union forces were retreating, the wounded sergeant was left behind, but Langbein refused to desert Mossman. He half-carried the large man for several miles, staggering under the weight, until a wagon driver gave them a ride. Finally, Mossman was taken to a Federal hospital in Roanoke.

When he recovered, Sergeant Mossman himself recommended the 15-year-old drummer for a Medal of Honor.

The other teen-age recipient of the Medal was George Hollat, 15, Third Class Boy aboard the U.S.S. *Varuna*. According to his citation, during an attack on Forts Jackson and St. Philip, April 24, 1862, "he rendered gallant service through the perilous action and remained steadfast and courageous at his battle station despite extremely heavy fire and the ramming of the *Varuna* by the rebel ship, *Morgan,* continuing his efforts until his ship, repeatedly holed and fatally damaged, was beached and sunk."

Among Medal winners of the Indian Wars were several full-blooded Indians who served as scouts for the Army. One of these bore what is probably the oddest name in the annals of the Medal of Honor: Co-Rux-Te-Chod-Ish (Mad Bear). He was a sergeant in the Pawnee Scouts. His exploit, and the justification for his award of the Medal are somewhat vague, but from the little information available it appears that he was given the Medal partly to placate him and other members of his tribe. During an engagement on the Republic River, Kansas, in 1869, Mad Bear apparently spotted a hostile Indian, ran out from his own unit in pursuit of the enemy and was shot and wounded by a bullet fired by one of his own company. No further comment is made in the official record. Another Indian scout by the name of Chiquito received the Medal and an equally brief citation. However, his exploits appear to have involved more positive accomplishment, for the citation reads, "Gallant conduct during campaigns and engagements with Apaches." 87

Dr. Mary E. Walker, Contract Surgeon

One of the oddest anecdotes regarding a Medal winner in the early days of the Award's establishment is so fantastic that it is worth describing at length. The recipient was an enterprising woman by the name of Dr. Mary Walker who became a contract surgeon for the Union Army.

The Civil War was at its height, and the nation was reeling from the news of bloody battles in 1863. In his Washington office Assistant Adjutant General Lt. Col. Edward D. Townsend, was absorbed in paper work when he was startled by a strange sight. He blinked and looked a second time at the figure standing before him. A woman with dark hair parted in the middle and severely drawn back was eyeing him coldly. The most surprising thing about her was her costume. She was wearing a man's suit, and stood stiffly, like an officer about to present his credentials.

"I wish an assignment in the Army as a field surgeon," she said abruptly.

Since in those days such a suggestion was as preposterous as the idea of rocketing to the moon, Townsend shook his head, incredulous at what he was seeing and hearing. Although Dr. Mary Edwards Walker explained that she had graduated from medical college and had been practicing medicine for eight years, Townsend tried in vain to dissuade her. Finally he shrugged and penned a note to the Surgeon General, recommending that he see what could be done for Dr. Walker.

The Surgeon General was not impressed. He flatly refused to give a woman a surgeon's commission. Angry but undismayed, Mary Walker accepted a job as a nurse in an army hospital. There she badgered the male doctors and surgeons, insisting that she could do their work, and refusing to perform many of the menial tasks expected of a nurse.

In November 1863, she wrote to Secretary of War Stanton, making an astonishing proposal. If she could be appointed regimental surgeon, she would take the responsibility of recruiting a regiment of men with criminal records. These men were to agree to enlist for the duration of the war. Although Stanton declined the offer, he highly commended her spirit and sent her to General Sherman with a letter asking him to use her as a doctor. Once again, Mary Walker was assigned to a hospital, but still she had no officer status.

Not satisfied, she now approached General George Thomas with a request that she be assigned to "special service," or espionage, with the 52nd Ohio Regiment. To General Thomas, who needed spies, and who had not experienced any previous contact with this obstreperous female doctor, it sounded like a perfectly acceptable request. But as usual, Mary's real motive was to gain a commission as an army surgeon. She had stipulated that she should be given such a commission as a cover for her spy activity!

However, General Thomas clearly stated that Dr. Walker was to be a "contract surgeon." This was a civilian post, with no officer status or military rank of any kind.

Evidently Mary Walker performed her duties as a spy with characteristic boldness. In April 1864, she was captured behind Confederate lines and spent four months at Libby Prison. She was released in a prisoner exchange in August, and went straightway to the man she had first approached for a commission, Colonel Edward Townsend, in Washington. There she announced that the Government owed her back pay for her service as an army officer.

General Thomas confirmed that she was due eighty dollars a month which she had earned as a contract surgeon, but this was quite a bit less than the officer pay she demanded. Still protesting, Mary Walker next appeared as doctor for the woman's section

of the military prison in Louisville, Ky. There she had some violent disagreements with a Dr. Brown, who supervised all medicine at the prison. When Dr. Brown ordered an investigation of her credentials to practice medicine, a highly prejudiced military medical board found her unqualified. They directed that she be discharged.

Soon the Civil War was ended, but not so Mary Walker's personal war against the Federal Government. She deluged War Department officials, generals and Congressmen with letters demanding recognition of her war service. Finally she went directly to Andrew Johnson. The President listened sympathetically to her amazing story, and was impressed by her sheaf of documents and letters. She told Johnson that she would cease her demands for back pay if he would give her the rank of major in the army.

As a result of this interview, President Johnson suggested that the Judge Advocate award Mary Walker a brevet commission, a commission giving a military officer higher nominal rank than that for which he receives pay. Since it turned out that this was not legally possible, Johnson asked Secretary Stanton to recognize Dr. Walker's services in some way. The order was passed on to Colonel Townsend, who by this time must have been willing to do almost any-

thing to rid himself of the woman's demands. In a memorandum to the War Department's chief clerk, he wrote, "The Secretary of War directs you have a Medal of Honor engraved by tomorrow for Dr. Mary E. Walker." The colonel presented the Medal on January 24, 1866.

Mary Walker continued to be a thorn in the Government's side for years. In 1871, she wrote a letter to Colonel Townsend asking him to inform the Commissioner of Pensions that she had been an Army contract surgeon in the Civil War. This Townsend agreed to do, but Dr. Walker was by no means satisfied. Convinced that a government pension was due her, she bombarded the War Department and other Government offices with letters, demands for copies of military orders, legal rulings and information that would support her claims. Finally, in 1876, Congress awarded her a pension of $8.50 a month.

But after a lifetime of battling male officials in Washington, her story reached an anticlimax. In 1916, when a Board of Review was appointed to examine all Medal of Honor citations, Dr. Walker's name was stricken from the roll. The fact remains, however, that Mary Edwards Walker held the distinction of being the only woman ever to wear the Medal of Honor.

89

Glossary

AMBUSCADE — an ambush; a place of concealment where troops wait to launch a surprise attack; a hidden body of troops.

ARMADA — a fleet of warships; the term now used to describe fleets of planes as well as ships.

B.A.R. — Browning automatic rifle used in World War II.

BARRAGE — a heavy concentration of artillery fire.

BATTALION — an army unit comprising two or more companies of infantry.

BATTLEWAGON — battleship, large warship; sometimes used in reference to large war planes and heavy bombers.

BAZOOKA — hand-operated rocket-launcher.

BELEAGUER — to surround and hold under siege.

BOLO — a large knife used both as a tool and a weapon by natives of the Philippine Islands.

BREECH HOLE — an opening in the breech, or loading end of a cannon, where a lighted match is inserted to set off the charge.

BREVET COMMISSION — an honorary rank; a promotion in rank without any increase in pay or authority.

BRIG — a prison or place of confinement aboard a ship.

BROADSIDE — the simultaneous firing of all guns along one side of a warship.

CAMOUFLAGE — concealment by means of coloring, shape or texture.

CANISTER — metal fragments, pieces or links of chain and other sharp objects discharged from a cannon. Shrapnel.

COLLIER — a ship employed in transporting coal.

COUNTERATTACK — an attack launched to stem an enemy offensive.

DEFILE — a narrow pass.

DOUGHBOY — the American foot soldier of World War I.

DREADNOUGHT — a large warship, usually of the battleship class.

EMPLACEMENT — a fortified gun position.

FLAK — the bursts and exploding fragments of anti-aircraft shells.

FLANK — (military) — one side of a body of troops, sometimes used as a verb meaning to seize a position on one side of an enemy force.

G.I. — An American soldier; also a term descriptive of any Army gear, weapons or equipment. Originated from the words, "Government Issue."

GENDARMERIE — a police force, drilled and trained for warfare.

GESTAPO — German secret police in World War II.

GRAPESHOT — pellets or bullet-like objects encased in a shell to provide a scatter charge when the shell explodes.

GRENADE — a small bomb designed to be thrown by hand and having a timing device to set it off seconds after it is tossed.

90

GUERRILLA — irregular war carried on by independent bands.

HOLOCAUST — a conflagration; wholesale destruction.

HOTCHKISS GUN — an air-cooled machine gun used in World War I.

HOWITZER — a type of cannon that fires shells at a steep trajectory.

LANYARD — a cord or line pulled to fire a cannon or artillery piece.

M-I RIFLE — a type of automatic rifle used by U.S. forces in World War II.

MM. — millimeter; .039 of an inch.

MACHETE — a large, heavy knife with a blade resembling a broad sword.

MASSACRE — a mass slaughter of people.

MATCHLOCK — an old type gun fired by a match applied to the powder charge.

MELEE — hand-to-hand combat.

MESSERSCHMIDT — a type of German fighter plane in World War II.

MORASS — a swamp or boggy region.

MORTAR — a short-tubed infantry weapon for close support. It is muzzle-loaded and fires at a high angle.

MUSKET — an early type of smooth bore gun, developed prior to the rifle.

MUZZLE — the mouth of a gun or cannon.

NIPA — a type of palm tree from the fronds of which thatched roofs are made.

NONCOM — a noncommissioned officer (corporal, sergeant) in the army.

OUTFLANK — to seize a strategic position to the left or right of the enemy force, generally forcing the enemy to withdraw.

PLATOON — a small body of military personnel functioning as a unit.

POTATO MASHER GRENADE — a type of hand grenade used by the Germans in World War I. The cylindrical grenade was attached to a wooden handle, making it look like a potato masher.

POWWOW — a conference; a term used primarily in reference to talks or meetings with North American Indians.

RAMPARTS — mounds or banks surrounding a fortified area.

RECONNOITER — to scout the area ahead of a main body of troops.

REDOUBT — a fortification, usually on a ridge or at the crest of a hill.

ROUND — (military) a single shell, charge or bullet fired from a gun.

S.S. TROOPS — German Storm Troopers in World War II, noted for their harsh discipline and identified by black uniforms.

SALIENT — an outward loop or wedge in a battle line, extending forward of the main body of troops.

SATCHEL CHARGE — several blocks of explosive usually taped to a board fitted with a rope or wire loop for use as a handle.

SHRAPNEL — fragments from exploding shells or grenades.

SIDESLIP — a sideways maneuver of an airplane, in which the pilot sends his plane downward to left or right.

STERNPOST — On a sailing vessel, a vertical beam to which the rudder is attached.

TILLER ROPE — a rope leading forward from either end of the tiller to the wheel or other steering device.

TROOPER — a cavalryman; an experienced soldier.

91

Index

ABBREVIATIONS FOR RANKS OF MEDAL OF HONOR WINNERS

Appr—Apprentice
Asst Surg—Assistant Surgeon
BM—Boatswain's Mate
BMC—Chief Boatswain's Mate
Brig Gen—Brigadier General
Capt—Captain
Capt Aft'gd—Captain of After Guard
Capt of Fo'c'sle—Captain of the Forecastle
Carp's Mate—Carpenter's Mate
Chap—Chaplain
Ch Bugler—Chief Bugler
Ch Carp's Mate—Chief Carpenter's Mate
Ch Mach—Chief Machinist
Col—Colonel
Col Sgt—Color Sergeant
Comis Sgt—Commissary Sergeant
Cpl—Corporal
Cox—Coxswain
Drum—Drummer
Elecn—Electrician
Eng's Cook—Engineer's Cook
FN—Fireman
GM—Gunner's Mate
Gy Sgt—Gunnery Sergeant
Hosp Appr—Hospital Apprentice
Hosp C—Hospital Corpsman
Hosp Man—Hospitalman
In Scout—Indian Scout
Lt—Lieutenant
Lt jg—Lieutenant Junior Grade
Lt Col—Lieutenant Colonel
Maj Gen—Major General
MAA—Master at Arms
MAAC—Chief Master at Arms
MMC—Chief Machinist's Mate
M/Sgt—Master Sergeant
Mus—Musician
Ord SN—Ordinary Seaman
Paym's Steward—Paymaster's Steward
Phar's Mate—Pharmacist's Mate
Pvt—Private
Pfc—Private First Class
Quar Gun—Quarter Gunner
QM—Quartermaster
QMC—Chief Quartermaster
R Adm—Rear Admiral
Sgt—Sergeant
Sfc—Sergeant First Class
Sgt Maj—Sergeant Major
Sig 1st C—Signalman First Class
Sig QM—Signal Quartermaster
SN—Seaman
Surg—Surgeon
T/Sgt—Technical Sergeant
T/4—Technician Fourth Class
YN—Yeoman
*Indicates a winner of more than one Award.

C. Dozier • Pfc Parker F. Dunn • Pfc Daniel R. Edwards • Sgt Alan Louis Eggers • Sgt Michael B. Ellis • Sgt Arthur J. Forrest • Sgt Gary Evans Foster • Pfc Jesse N. Funk • 1st Lt Harold A. Furlong • Pfc Frank Gaffney • 1st Lt Harold Ernest Goettler • Sgt Earl D. Gregory • 1st Sgt Sydney G. Gumpertz • Sgt Thomas Lee Hall • Sgt M. Waldo Hatler • 1st Lt George Price Hays • Cpl James D. Heriot • Cpl Ralyn M. Hill • Sgt Richmond H. Hilton • Capt Nelson M. Holderman • Pfc Harold I. Johnston • Sgt James E. Karnes • Sgt Phillip C. Katz • 1st Sgt Benjamin Kaufman • Sgt John Cridland Latham • 1st Sgt Milo Lemert • Pvt

Berger Loman • 2nd Lt Frank Luke, Jr. • Capt George H. Mallon • Cpl Sidney E. Manning • Capt George G. McMurtry • Sgt James I. Mestrovitch • Capt L. Wardlaw Miles • Maj Oscar F. Miller • Pvt Sterling Morelock • Pvt Thomas C. Neibaur • Sgt Richard W. O'Neil • Cpl Thomas E. O'Shea • 2nd Lt Samuel I. Parker • Pvt Archie A. Peck • Pfc Michael J. Perkins • Lt Col Emory J. Pike • Cpl Thomas A. Pope • 2nd Lt Patrick Regan • 1st Lt Edward V. Rickenbacker • 1st Lt George S. Robb • Cpl Harold W. Roberts • Cpl Samuel M. Sampler • Sgt Willie Sandlin • Sgt William Sawelson • 1st Lt Dwite H. Schaffner • Sgt Lloyd M. Seibert • Capt Alexander R. Skinker • Pvt Clayton K. Slack • Lt Col Fred E. Smith • Sgt Edward R. Talley • Maj Joseph H. Thompson • Cpl Harold L. Turner • 1st Lt William B. Turner • Pvt Michael Valente • Sgt Ludovicus M. M. Van Iersel • Cpl John C. Villepigue • Sgt Reidar Waaler • Pvt Calvin John Ward • 1st Sgt Chester H. West • Maj Charles W. Whittlesey • 2nd Lt J. Hunter Wickersham • Pvt Nels Wold • 1st Lt Samuel Woodfill • Cpl Alvin C. York . . . . NAVY — Phar's Mate 1st C John Henry Balch • Lt Joel Thompson Boone • Com Willis Winter Bradley, Jr. • SN Tedford H. Cann • Ship's Cook 3rd C Jessie Whitfield Covington • SN Ora Graves • Hosp. App 1st C David E. Hayden • GM1 Osmond K. Ingram • Lt Edouard Victor Michael Izac • Lt Com Alexander Gordon Lyle • BMC John MacKenzie • Ship's Fitter 1st C Patrick McGunigal • MMC Francis Edward Ormsbee, Jr. • Lt jg Weedon E. Osborne • GMC Oscar Schmidt, Jr. • BM2 John Otto Siegel • QM Frank Monroe Upton . . . . NAVAL RESERVE FORCE — Ensign Charles Hazeltine Hammann • Lt Com James Jonas Madison • Lt Orlando Henderson Petty • Ensign Daniel Augustus Joseph Sullivan . . . . . . MARINE CORPS — *Sgt Louis Cukela • Gy Sgt Charles F. Hoffman • *Gy Sgt Ernest August Janson • *Pvt John Joseph Kelly • *Sgt Matej Kocak • *Cpl John Henry Pruitt • Gy Sgt Robert Guy Robinson • Gy Sgt Fred W. Stockham • 2nd Lt Ralph Talbot . . . . . 2ND NICARAGUAN CAMPAIGN, MARINE CORPS — 1st Lt Christian Frank Schilt • Cpl Donald LeRoy Truesdell . . . . INTERIM CITATIONS, 1920, NAVY — Lt Com William M. Corry, Jr. . . . . . . 1921, USMC — Pvt Albert Joseph Smith . . . . 1922, USN — Lt Com Walter Atlee Edwards . . . . 1923, NAVY — Torpedoman 2nd C Henry Breault • MM William Russell Huber • Ensign Thomas J. Ryan . . . . 1924, USN — BM1 George Robert Cholister • Ensign Henry Clay Drexler . . . . . . 1926, NAVY — Mach Floyd Bennett • Com Richard Evelyn Byrd, Jr. . . . . . . 1927, NAVY — GMC Thomas Eadie . . . . . USA — Capt Charles A. Lindbergh . . . . . 1935, USA — Maj Gen Ret Adolphus W. Greely . . . . . 1938, NAVY — Lt Carlton B Hutchins . . . . 1939, NAVY — MMC William Badders • BMC Orson L. Crandall • Ch Metalsmith James Harper McDonald • Torpedoman 1st C John Mihalowski . . . . WORLD WAR II, ARMY — S/Sgt Lucian Adams • T/Sgt Beauford T. Anderson • Sgt Sylvester Antolak • Pfc Thomas E. Atkins . . . . . . Sgt Thomas A. Baker • 2nd Lt Van T. Barfoot • Pvt Carlton W. Barrett • 1st Lt Raymond O Beaudoin • T/Sgt Bernard P. Bell • S/Sgt Stanley Bender • Pfc George Benjamin, Jr. • Cpl Edward A. Bennett • M/Sgt Veto R. Bertoldo • Cpl Arthur O. Beyer • Pfc Melvin E. Biddle • 1st Lt Arnold L. Bjorklund • 1st Lt Orville E. Block • S/Sgt Paul L. Bolden • 1st Lt Cecil H. Bolton • Pvt Robert D. Booker • 2nd Lt George W. G. Boyce, Jr. • S/Sgt Hershel F. Briles • Capt Maurice L. Britt • Pfc Leonard C. Brostrom • Capt Bobbie E. Brown • 1st Lt Frank Burke • 1st Sgt Elmer J. Burr • Pfc Herbert H. Burr • Capt James M. Burt • 2nd Lt John E. Butts . . . . . S/Sgt Alvin P. Carey • T/Sgt Charles F. Carey, Jr. • Pfc Joseph J. Cicchetti • 2nd Lt Ernest Childers • S/Sgt Clyde L. Choate • 2nd Lt Dale Eldon Christensen • Pfc Herbert F. Christian • T/Sgt Francis J. Clark • Pfc Mike Colalillo • Lt Col Robert G. Cole • Sgt James P. Connor • S/Sgt Raymond H. Cooley • T/Sgt Charles H. Coolidge • Pfc Richard Eller Cowan • Pfc Clarence B. Craft • 2nd Lt Robert Craig • T/Sgt Morris E. Crain • Pvt William J. Crawford • S/Sgt John R. Crews • Sgt Francis S. Currey . . . . . 2nd Lt Edward C. Dahlgren • T/Sgt Peter J. Dalessondro • Capt Michael J. Daly • Maj Charles W. Davis • S/Sgt Arthur F. De Franzo • Pfc Charles N. De Glopper • Sgt Emile Deleau, Jr. • 2nd Lt Ernest H. Dervishian • Pfc James H. Diamond • S/Sgt Robert H. Dietz • Pfc Desmond T. Doss • S/Sgt Jessie R. Drowley • T/Sgt Russell E. Dunham • Pfc John W. Dutko . . . . . S/Sgt Walter D. Ehlers • S/Sgt Gerald L. Endl • Sgt Ray E. Eubanks • T/Sgt Forrest E. Everhart . . . . . 1st Lt James H. Fields • 1st Lt Almond E. Fisher • Sgt William G. Fournier • 2nd Lt Thomas W. Fowler • Pvt Elmer E. Fryar • 1st Sgt Leonard A. Funk, Jr. . . . . Capt William Wylie Galt • S/Sgt Archer T. Gammon • S/Sgt Marcario Garcia • Pvt Harold A. Garman • T/Sgt Robert E. Gerstung • T/5 Eric G. Gibson • Pfc David M. Gonzales • Pfc William J. Grabiarz • 2nd Lt Stephen R. Gregg • Sgt Kenneth E. Gruennert . . . . . . S/Sgt George J. Hall • T/5 Lewis Hall • S/Sgt Sherwood H. Hallman • Sgt Roy W. Harmon • Cpl Harry R. Harr • 2nd Lt James L. Harris • Pfc Joe R. Hastings • Sgt John D. Hawk • Pfc Lloyd C. Hawks • T/Sgt Clinton M. Hedrick • S/Sgt James M. Hendrix • Pvt Robert T. Henry • Pfc Silvestre S. Herrera • S/Sgt Freeman V. Horner • Cpl Paul B. Huff • . . . . . . S/Sgt Isadore S. Jachman • Pvt Elden H. Johnson • Sgt Leroy Johnson • Sgt Oscar G. Johnson, Jr. • Pfc William J. Johnston . . . . . . 1st Lt Victor L. Kandle • Sgt Christos H. Karaberis • S/Sgt George D. Keathley • S/Sgt Gus Kerfurt • S/Sgt Jonah E. Kelley • Pvt Ova A. Kelley • Cpl Charles E. Kelly • T/Sgt John D. Kelly • Cpl Thomas J. Kelly • Pfc Dexter J. Kerstetter • Pfc Patrick L. Kessler • T/4 Truman Kimbro • Pvt Harold G. Kiner • 2nd Lt Gerry H. Kisters • Pfc Alton W. Knappenberger • 1st Lt Jack L. Knight • Pfc Anthony L. Krotiak . . . . . S/Sgt Robert E. Laws • 1st Lt Daniel W. Lee • 1st Lt Turney W. Leonard • T/Sgt Jake W. Lindsey • Pfc Floyd K. Lindstrom • 1st Lt Edgar H. Lloyd • Pvt Donald R. Lobaugh • Sgt James M. Logan • Sgt Jose M. Lopez . . . . . . Lt Col George L. Mabry, Jr. • Com Gen Douglas MacArthur • Sgt Charles A. MacGillivary • Pfc John D. Magrath • Pfc Joe E. Mann • Pvt Joe P. Martinez • T/5 Robert D. Maxwell • Pfc Martin O. May • Cpl Melvin Mayfield • S/Sgt Thomas E. McCall • Pvt Lloyd G. McCarter • M/Sgt Charles L. McGaha • T/Sgt Vernon McGarity • Pvt William D. McGee • Sgt Troy A. McGill • Pfc Francis X. McGraw • Sgt John R. McKinney • Sgt John J. McVeigh • Pfc William A. McWhorter • T/Sgt John Meagher • Pfc Gino J. Merli • Pvt Joseph F. Marrell • Sgt Harold O. Messerschmidt • 2nd Lt Harry J. Michael • S/Sgt Andrew Miller • Pvt James H. Mills • S/Sgt John W. Minick • Pvt Nicholas Minue • 1st Lt Jimmie W. Monteith, Jr. • 1st Lt Jack C. Montgomery • Pvt Harold H. Moon, Jr. • Pfc Edward J. Moskala • Sgt Charles E. Mower • Sgt Joseph E. Muller • Pfc Sadao S. Munemori • 1st Lt Audie L. Murphy • Pfc Frederick C. Murphy • 1st Lt Charles P. Murray, Jr. . . . . . . Sgt William L. Nelson • Sgt Ralph G. Neppel • Capt Robert B. Nett • 1st Lt Beryl R. Newman . . . . Lt Col William J. O'Brien • 1st Lt Carlos C. Ogden • Capt Arlo L. Olson • Sgt Truman O. Olson • M/Sgt Nicholas Oresko . . . . . . T/4 Laverne Parrish • T/5 Forrest E. Peden • S/Sgt Jack J. Pendleton • T/Sgt Frank D. Peregory • Pfc Manuel Perez, Jr. • Pvt George J. Peters • S/Sgt George Peterson • Pfc Frank J. Petrarca • T/5 John J. Pinder • Pfc Leo J. Powers • Pfc Ernest W. Prussman . . . . . . 1st Lt Bernard J. Ray • Pvt James W. Reese • Pvt John N. Reese, Jr. • 2nd Lt Paul F. Riordan • 1st Lt James E. Robinson, Jr. • T/Sgt Cleto Rodriguez • Capt Robert E. Roeder • Brig Gen Theodore Roosevelt, Jr. • Pfc Wilburn K. Ross • 2nd Lt Donald E. Rudolph • Sgt Alejandro R. Ruiz . . . . . . Sgt Joseph J. Sadowski • Pfc Foster J. Sayers • S/Sgt Joseph E. Schaefer • Pfc Henry Schauer • Capt Robert S. Scott • 2nd Lt Charles W. Shea • Pfc Carl V. Sheridan • Pfc William R. Shockley • S/Sgt Curtis F. Shoup • 1st Lt Edward A. Silk • S/Sgt John C. Sjogren • Cpl James D. Slaton • Pvt Furman L. Smith • Pfc William A. Soderman • Sgt Joe C. Specker • S/Sgt Junior J. Spurrier • Sgt John C. Squires • Pfc Stuart S. Stryker • Capt Seymour W. Terry • Pfc William H. Thomas • Sgt Max Thompson • Cpl Horace M. Thorne • Pfc John F. Thorson • 1st Lt John J. Tominac • Pvt John R. Towle • Capt Jack L. Treadwell • Sgt Day G. Turner • Pfc George B. Turner . . . . . . Pfc Jose F. Valdez • Pvt Junior Van Noy • 2nd Lt Robert M. Viale • S/Sgt Ysmael R. Villegas • Pfc Dirk J. Vlug . . . . . . Gen Jonathan M. Wainwright • Pfc Herman C. Wallace • Lt Col Keith L. Ware • Cpl Henry F. Warner • 1st Lt Robert T. Waugh • 1st Lt David C. Waybur • Sgt Ellis R. Weicht • Pfc Walter C. Wetzel • 1st Lt Eli Whiteley • Sgt Hulon B. Whittington • S/Sgt Paul J. Wiedorfer • 2nd Lt Thomas W. Wigle • Col William H. Wilbur • Cpl Edward G. Wilkin • 1st Lt Walter J. Will • T/5 Alfred L. Wilson • S/Sgt Homer L. Wise • S/Sgt Howard E. Woodford . . . . . . Pvt Rodger W. Young . . . . 2nd Lt Raymond Zussman . . . . . . AIR CORPS — Lt Col Addison E. Baker • Maj Richard I. Bong • Maj Horace S. Carswell, Jr. • Brig Gen